民航实用英语
听力教程（下册）

主　编◎王　莹　李雯艳
副主编◎邓丽君　刘艳妮　黄　晨　倪欣雨

Practical English Listening Course for Aviation Service
(Volume Two)

清华大学出版社
北京

内容简介

《民航实用英语听力教程》分为上下两册，一共 14 个单元，每个单元均包括以下几方面：语感热身、听力基础技巧训练、客舱服务过程中涉及的对话、段落理解以及文化赏析等。《民航实用英语听力教程（下册）》以民航乘务服务中的常规活动为主题，内容涉及民航服务的各个方面，比如餐饮服务、转机、海关安检等内容。每单元都设置多个服务片段或情境，将语言学习贯穿其中，并适当拓展旅行及民航的相关知识，素材丰富，体裁多样，语言规范。

本书适合空中乘务专业的学生使用，同时也适用于对空乘服务行业感兴趣的业余爱好者。本着因材施教和个性化教学的原则，教师在教学时可以针对学时设置和学生的具体接受程度来决定教学过程的安排并对教材内容进行选择。

本书封面贴有清华大学出版社防伪标签，无标签者不得销售。
版权所有，侵权必究。举报：010-62782989，beiqinquan@tup.tsinghua.edu.cn。

图书在版编目（CIP）数据

民航实用英语听力教程. 下册 / 王莹，李雯艳主编. —北京：清华大学出版社，2022.7
ISBN 978-7-302-61076-2

Ⅰ. ①民… Ⅱ. ①王… ②李… Ⅲ. ①民用航空—英语—听说教学—高等学校—教材 Ⅳ. ①F56

中国版本图书馆CIP数据核字（2022）第 098186 号

责任编辑：杜春杰
封面设计：刘　超
版式设计：文森时代
责任校对：马军令
责任印制：曹婉颖

出版发行：清华大学出版社
　　　　网　　址：http://www.tup.com.cn，http://www.wqbook.com
　　　　地　　址：北京清华大学学研大厦 A 座　　邮　　编：100084
　　　　社 总 机：010-83470000　　邮　　购：010-62786544
　　　　投稿与读者服务：010-62776969，c-service@tup.tsinghua.edu.cn
　　　　质量反馈：010-62772015，zhiliang@tup.tsinghua.edu.cn
印 装 者：北京嘉实印刷有限公司
经　　销：全国新华书店
开　　本：185mm×260mm　　印　张：9.5　　字　数：221 千字
版　　次：2022 年 7 月第 1 版　　印　次：2022 年 7 月第 1 次印刷
定　　价：39.80 元

产品编号：077344-01

前　言

　　《民航实用英语听力教程（下册）》的编写以教育部关于空中乘务专业的要求和中国民航总局关于空乘人员的素质、能力要求为依据，遵循系统性、适用性、实践性和前瞻性的原则，旨在培养高素质、专业化的民航空乘专业的服务人才。在设计和编写中，本教材借鉴了近年来大学英语教学的成功经验及教学成果，汲取了国内外先进的教学理念与教学方法，并充分考虑到了本专业教学对象的学习特点以及学生对于职业与专业发展的需要。

　　通过对本教材的学习与应用，学生将在不断提高外语能力的同时，使自身的综合职业素养、专业服务意识与技能得以全面提升。在模拟情景中，学生将不断地历练职场的心理适应能力和承受能力，也会获得较高水准的解决突发事件的能力，这使他们可以在空乘职业生涯中尽显风采，成为国际型服务人才。

　　本教材每单元均包括以下四个部分，具体编排如下。

　　1. Pre-listening。课前准备主要包括两个部分：一部分是名言警句、笑话、谜语、绕口令等内容，或俗语谚语、固定搭配等资料；另一部分主要是语音知识和听力技巧的介绍，为提高学生的听力打下良好的基础。课前准备意在培养学生的语感，使学生感受语言的魅力，提高学习兴趣，并且能够较快进入学习状态。

　　2. Listening In。这部分包括两个板块，一块是按照英语考试的问答形式设置练习；另一块为与本单元主题相关的空乘服务过程中涉及的对话及行业用语，配以多种形式的习题。

　　3. Listening and Understanding。此部分主要是与本单元主题相关的航空公司的管理规定，或者航空方面的一些相关知识及信息介绍等。

　　4. Listening and Enjoying。此部分主要以文化为主题，拓宽学生视野，使学生欣赏英语并感受英语语言的魅力，同时了解各种文化，培养跨文化交际能力。

　　本教材通过生动的听力材料、逼真的情景再现，使学生了解空中乘务工作所涉及的各个层面，培养学生扎实的英语语言基础和较强的英语综合应用能力。

　　根据学生学习的特点，为适应教师教学需求，本教材在编排上有如下特点。

　　1. 在结构上，本教材围绕每单元的主题进行听说的能力训练，有侧重，有统一，实用又适用。各板块循序渐进，相辅相成，帮助学生养成良好的学习习惯，提高自主学习能力。

　　2. 在选材上，本教材尽量收集并编排近年来的最新资料，同时适当添加了托福英语考试的部分形式让学生了解，并增添了培养语感的谜语、笑话及文化赏析等内容，选材涵盖面广，内容丰富，角度新颖，语言地道实用。

　　3. 在原则上，针对本专业学生的特点、培养目标和教学特色，各部分的编写都旨在突出培养学生英语语言的实用能力和交际能力，同时强化专业技能与素养。

　　4. 在内容上，本教材充分注意课堂教学与课外自主学习相结合，既有大量的专业知识，同时也辅以能够提高语感的谜语、绕口令等内容，还有能够感受文化背景和文化差异的人文性文章，专业内容以对话、采访、情境模拟等多种形式体现，并配有多种习题。

5．在技术上，本教材充分利用现代信息技术，特意采用新式的二维码技术代替光盘，为英语网络化及现代化教学提供了便利，同时也大大方便学生自主学习。

本教材由教学经验丰富的一线英语教师编写，跨校横向合作，并聘请航空公司有多年从业经验的乘务人员参与编写与指导，其中第十三单元由王莹老师编写，第八单元由刘艳妮老师编写，第九单元由黄晨老师编写，第十一单元由邓丽君老师编写，第十、十二、十四单元由王莹、倪欣雨老师共同编写。在编写过程中，各位老师坚持做到职业性、实用性、专业性和趣味性统一，重在培养学生在职业工作环境下较强的英语实际应用能力，向行业输送国际型的空乘服务人才。本教材的编写得到了许多朋友的关心、帮助和指导。清华大学出版社的编辑们在整套教材的策划、编写、版式设计、配图等方面做了大量的工作。在此，编者对大家的辛苦付出表示诚挚的感谢。

本教材如有不当和疏漏之处，敬请各位专家、同仁、读者批评指正，以便我们不断地完善和提高。

编者
2021 年 10 月

CONTENTS 目录

Unit 8 ··· 1

    Part I   Pre-listening ·· 2
        Matching ··· 2
        Pronunciation ··· 2
    Part II   Listening In ··· 4
        Responses ··· 4
        Dialogue: Serving the Food ··· 4
        Dialogue: Serving the Drink ·· 5
    Part III   Listening and Understanding ··· 6
        Passage: Mobile Phones are Allowed on Planes — For or Against? ························ 6
        Passage: C919, Chinese-made Airbus, Our National Pride ································· 7
    Part IV   Listening and Enjoying ·· 9
        Cultural Perspective: Dining Etiquette in Western Country ······························· 9
        A Poem: I remember, I remember ··· 9

Unit 9 ··· 11

    Part I   Pre-listening ··· 12
        Tongue Twister ·· 12
        Pronunciation ·· 12
    Part II   Listening In ··· 13
        Responses ··· 13
        Dialogue: Supplementary Reading Material ·· 14
        Dialogue: How to Use the Headsets? ·· 15
    Part III   Listening and Understanding ··· 15
        Dialogue: Lift the Screen up ··· 15
        Passage: The Entertainment System ··· 17
        Passage: Notting Hill ··· 18

Part IV　Listening and Enjoying ·· 19
　　Cultural Perspective: Peking Opera ·· 19
　　Friends: The One with the Proposal ··· 20

Unit 10 ·· 22

Part I　Pre-listening ··· 23
　　Idioms ·· 23
　　Pronunciation ·· 23
　　Abbreviation ··· 23
Part II　Listening In ·· 24
　　Responses ··· 24
　　Duty-free Announcement on Board ·· 25
　　Dialogue: Price for Items ·· 25
　　Dialogue: Souvenirs and Gifts on Board ·· 26
Part III　Listening and Understanding ··· 27
　　Dialogue: In-flight Sales ··· 27
　　Passage: Some Rules on In-flight Duty-free Purchase in CSA ···································· 27
Part IV　Listening and Enjoying ··· 29
　　Star Alliance ··· 29
　　Yoga ··· 30

Unit 11 ·· 31

Part I　Pre-listening ··· 32
　　Tongue Twisters ··· 32
　　Pronunciation ·· 32
　　Intonation ··· 33
Part II　Listening In ·· 34
　　Responses ··· 34
　　Dialogue: Service for Special Passengers ·· 34
　　Dialogue: Check-in for Special Passengers ··· 35
　　Dialogue: Passenger with an Infant ·· 36
Part III　Listening and Understanding ··· 37
　　Dialogue: Upgrading ·· 37
　　Passage: Assistance for Incapacitated Passengers ·· 37
Part IV　Listening and Enjoying ··· 38
　　Some Famous Airports in the World ·· 38

Unit 12 ... 41

Part I Pre-listening ... 42
Slangs ... 42
Pronunciation ... 42

Part II Listening In ... 43
Responses ... 43
Dialogues: Medical Problems ... 43
Announcement: Sudden Emergency Announcement ... 44
Dialogue: The Injured Passenger on Board ... 44
Dialogue: Is there a Doctor on Board? ... 45

Part III Listening and Understanding ... 46
Dialogue: Emergency commands ... 46
Announcement: Preparing for an Emergency Evacuation ... 46

Part IV Listening and Enjoying ... 47
Passage: Film on Pilot's Heroic Story to Begin Shooting ... 47
Culture Perspective: Tennis Tournaments ... 48

Unit 13 ... 50

Part I Pre-listening ... 51
Opposites ... 51
Pronunciation ... 51

Part II Listening In ... 52
Responses ... 52
Dialogue: My Luggage in Connecting Flight ... 52
Passage: Why Book Your Airport Transfer with Us? ... 53
Dialogue: Free Singapore Bus Tour During Your Transit ... 54

Part III Listening and Understanding ... 55
Dialogue: Unaccompanied Minor Lounges For Connection ... 55
Passage: A Transit Visa ... 56

Part IV Listening and Enjoying ... 57
Recruitment ... 57
Cultural Perspective: Iceland ... 58

Unit 14 ... 59

Part I Pre-listening ... 60
Puzzles ... 60

　　　　Pronunciation ··· 60
　Part II　Listening In ·· 61
　　　　Responses ··· 61
　　　　Questions: General Information about CIQ ································ 61
　　　　Dialogue: My Customs Declaration ··· 62
　　　　Dialogue: China Immigration Clearance ···································· 63
　Part III　Listening and Understanding ·· 63
　　　　Passage: Peoples Republic of China Duty Free Allowances Summary ········· 63
　　　　Passage: Macau Duty Free Allowances Summary ·························· 64
　Part IV　Listening and Enjoying ·· 65
　　　　Passage: European airlines ··· 65
　　　　Culture Perspective: Hulun Buir Grassland ································ 66

Keys and Audio scripts ·· 67
Bibliography ·· 136
Appendix ·· 137

Unit 8
Meal and Drink Service

Part I Pre-listening

Matching

Listen to the following sentences and match them with the pictures below.

(1) [   ]   (2) [   ]

(3) [   ]   (4) [   ]

(5) [   ]   (6) [   ]

From *Peppa Pig: The Holiday House*

Pronunciation

I. Directions: The following boxes are going to introduce four types of the loss of plosives. You'll hear four groups of words and then try to underline where the loss of plosives occurs.

> When a plosive is close to another one, the loss of plosive happens in the former. Six plosives include: /p/ /b/ /t/ /d/ /k/ /g/
> Example: O<u>c</u>tober
> /ɒ<u>k</u>'təʊbə/

practice   September   goodbye
update   cocktail   looked

> When a plosive is close to fricative consonant, the incomplete loss of plosive happens. Ten fricative consonants include: /f/ /v/ /s/ /z/ /ʃ/ /ʒ/ /θ/ /ð/ /r/ /h/
> Example: as<u>k</u> for
> /ɑ:s<u>k</u> 'fɔ:/

exist   advice   accept
success   friendship   bookshelf

> When a plosive is close to affricates, the incomplete loss of plosive happens. Two affricates include: /tʃ/ /dʒ/
> Example: har<u>d</u> job
> /hɑr<u>d</u> dʒɔb/

picture   lecture   object
subject   a good job   best choice

> When a plosive is close to nasals, the incomplete loss of plosive happens. Three nasals include: /m/ /n/ /ŋ/
> Example: a<u>t</u> night
> /æ<u>t</u> nait/

admit   nickname   sudden
certain   midnight   department

II. Directions: Listen to the following sentences and underline where the loss of plosives occurs.

1. Teacher asks us to write down our names on the blackboard.
2. When you have free time, please stop by for a chat.
3. Chinese culture is quite different from western culture.
4. When I see these old photos, I always think of my childhood.
5. Do you like deep red or light red?
6. I think this is a good chance to improve your ability.
7. Great changes have taken place in China.
8. It is really a pleasant journey with you.
9. The prince and princess finally got married and lived happily.
10. Lucy and Lily are my old friends.

Part II Listening In

Responses

You will hear five sentences. Listen carefully and select the best response to the questions or statements.

1. A. Yes, it's advisable.
   B. pleasure.
   C. You don't need to think so.
2. A. Sorry, I won't.
   B. Keep doing like this.
   C. You will be fined.
3. A. Please fill out some forms and bring your ID card.
   B. It takes you about forty minutes to get our club.
   C. Our services are the best.
4. A. After that lunch, I am not sure I can eat anything!
   B. Take it easy.
   C. Hurry up, will you?
5. A. Don't mention it!
   B. Sounds good!
   C. Don't look at me.

Dialogue: Serving the Food

Word Study

snack: a small meal or amount of food, usually eaten in a hurry

tray table: flat piece of wood, metal, plastic, etc. table used for holding things

vegetarian: person who eats no meat

muslim: someone who believes in Islam and lives according to its rules

stew: to cook slowly and for a long time in liquid

greasy: containing an unusual amount of oil

shrimp: small shellfish with long tails and many legs

I. Listen to the dialogue and try to tell whether the following statements are true or not.

1. The passenger asks the flight attendant about the time for taking off. (   )

2. The passenger has put down his tray table already before the flight attendant tells to do so. (   )

3. The passenger will remember to order a special meal next time. (   )

4. The passenger finally chose fruits salad because he likes the greasy food. (   )

5. The flight attendant solved the problem the passenger complained about. (   )

II. Listen to the dialogue again and choose the proper answer to the questions.

1. How long does the flight attendant begin to serve dinner after take-off?

    A. 13 minutes.   B. 30 minutes.   C. 40 minutes.   D. 60 minutes.

2. What kinds of food does the flight attendant promise to bring to the passenger as soon as the plane takes off?

    A. Some drinks.   B. Some salads.   C. Some desserts.   D. Some snacks.

3. How many main dishes does the flight offer?

    A. One.   B. Two.   C. Three.   D. Four.

4. Why does the passenger finally decide to have fruits salad instead of vegetable salad?

    A. He is a vegetarian.

    B. He is on the diet.

    C. He doesn't like shrimp.

    D. He thinks fruits are fresher than vegetables.

5. The passenger complains about the services **EXCEPT** that _____.

    A. the attendant keeps passenger waiting too long

    B. the fruits in this salad are not fresh

    C. the salad is too dry

    D. the chicken is all burned

Dialogue: Serving the Drink

Word Study

thirsty: feeling a need or desire to drink

interrupt: to make a break in someone's activity

available: obtainable or accessible and ready for use or service

destination: the place designated as the end

typical: exhibiting the qualities or characteristics that identify a group or kind or category

I. Listen to the following dialogue and choose the proper answer to the question.

1. According to the dialogue, what kind of drink is **NOT** served on the plane?

    A. Coffee.   B. Beer.   C. Juice.   D. Tea.

2. What was the man doing while the drink served?

    A. Eating.   B. Reading.   C. Sleeping.   D. Chatting.

3. Why does the man choose tea?
    A. Because he has drunk tea before.
    B. Because he likes to try something different.
    C. Because he likes to try something typically Chinese.
    D. Because he likes to try something sour.
4. What kinds of tea does the second man finally order?
    A. Dragon Well tea.   B. Biluochun.   C. Black tea.   D. Green tea.
5. If people want to lose weight, they should try _____.
    A. Dragon Well tea   B. Biluochun   C. Black tea   D. Green tea

II. Listen to the dialogue again and then fill in the blanks.
1. I'm a little _____ now.
2. I didn't want to _____ you.
3. Well, what is _____ on board?
4. I want to have something _____.
5. Since our _____ is Beijing, I'd like to try something typically Chinese.

Part III Listening and Understanding

Passage: Mobile Phones are Allowed on Planes — For or Against?

Word Study

domestic: of concern to or concerning the internal affairs of a nation

permit: to allow

portable: easily or conveniently transported

switch on: to turn on

represent: to be a symbol

violate: to fail to agree with

uncivilized: not behaving in a way that is correct according to social or normal standards

chaos: a state of extreme confusion and disorder

awareness: having knowledge of

acceptable: agreed by most people in a society

authority: the power or right to give orders or make decisions

lay down: to establish a rule that people should obey

regulate: to give direction to

maintain: to keep in safety and protect from harm, decay, loss, or destruction

Unit 8 Meal and Drink Service

I. Listen to the passage and try to tell whether the following statements are true or not.

1. The new rule allows passengers to use their phones on the plane but they have airplane mode switched on . (   )
2. Most domestic routes have been equipped with Wi-Fi services. (   )
3. It doesn't matter that passengers watch videos without using earphones. (   )
4. People have already known what they should do in flight so authorities don't need make rules. (   )
5. Passenger and authorities should make joint efforts to maintain order during the flight. (   )

II. Listen to the passage again and try to finish the summary.

> **Topic: Mobile Phones are Allowed on Planes**
>
> **For**
> • making flying more 1._____
> • represent huge 2._____
>
> **Against**
> • some behaviors that 3._____ the rights of others
> • some behaviors that are more likely to lead to 4._____ or 5._____
>
> **Suggestions**
> • passengers should 6._____ what can be done during the flight
> • authorities should 7._____ some rules
>
> **Effects**
> • People's behavior on airplanes should be 8._____ and legal rights can be 9._____
> • public order can be 10._____

Passage: C919, Chinese-made Airbus, Our National Pride

> **Word Study**
>
> maiden: unmarried woman
> aviation: design and manufacture of aircraft
> option: choice
> dominate: to have control or a very strong influence on people or events
> mature: fully grown or developed
> innovation: making changes; introducing new things

7

> breakthrough: an important development or achievement
> economical: careful in the spending of money, time, etc. and in the use of resources; not wasteful
> competitive: of or involving competition
> roll off: to allow vehicles to be driven off
> assembly: act or process of fitting together the parts of something
> assessment: consideration of someone or something and a judgment about them

I. Listen to the passage and match the information in the box with the following sentences.

a. Boeing and Airbus
b. China
c. Airbus 320 and Boeing 737
d. 23 foreign and domestic customers
e. C919

1. (   ) the first large passenger aircraft designed and built by China.
2. (   ) very mature aircraft manufacturers.
3. (   ) have placed orders for 570 aircraft.
4. (   ) currently dominate the market.
5. (   ) has invested heavily in commercial passenger jet manufacturing.

II. Listen to the dialogue again and try to tell whether the following statements are true or not.

1. Jet C919 has more than 150 seats. (   )
2. Jet C919 finally landed on the Shanghai Pudong International Airport. (   )
3. Jet C919 had become a strong competitor with the updated Airbus 320 and 737. (   )
4. In November 2007, the first C919 jet rolled off the assembly line. (   )
5. The last step before a plane maiden flight is technical assessment. (   )

III. Listen to the dialogue again and choose the proper answer to the question.

1. The flight has great importance in many aspects **EXCEPT** that _____.
   A. it means a significant step for Chinese aviation industry.
   B. it is the first large passenger aircraft designed and built by China.
   C. it offers a strong option for global carriers in decades to come.
   D. it has become a mature aircraft manufacturer.

2. Which one is not the feature of C919?
   A. It focuses on innovation.
   B. It focuses on technological breakthroughs.
   C. It is economical and comfortable.

D. It currently dominates the market.
3. According to the passage, which kind of airplane is invested heavily in China?
   A. Military jet manufacturing.
   B. Goods delivery jet manufacturing.
   C. Commercial passenger jet manufacturing.
   D. Private jet manufacturing.
4. How long does the technical assessment usually take?
   A. One to two days.
   B. One to two weeks.
   C. One to two months.
   D. One to two years.
5. If customers want to purchase the C919, who can they find to ask for?
   A. State Council.
   B. China's national carrier Air China.
   C. Boeing and Airbus.
   D. Commercial Aircraft Corporation of China (COMAC).

Part IV　Listening and Enjoying

Cultural Perspective: Dining Etiquette in Western Country

Listen to the passage and try to tell whether the following statements are true or not.

1. A plate is placed in the middle and forks should be arranged to the right of the plate while knives should be placed to the left. (　)
2. A full course dinner usually consists of starter, main course and dessert. (　)
3. Bread is the main ingredient in the main course. (　)
4. White wine should go with white meat while the red wine should go with red meat. (　)
5. It is impolite to arrive 10 to 15 minutes later than the appointed time to dinner at home in England. (　)

A Poem: I remember, I remember

I remember, I remember

by Thomas Hood

I remember, I remember,
The house where I was born,

The little window where the sun,
Came peeping in at morn;
He never came a wink too soon,
Nor brought too long a day,
But now I often wish the night,
Had borne my breath away!

I remember, I remember,
The roses red and white,
The violets, and the lily-cups,
Those flowers made of light!
The lilacs where the robin built,
And where my brother set,
The laburnum on his birth-day,
The tree is living yet!

I remember, I remember,
Where I was used to swing,
And thought the air must rush as fresh,
To swallows on the wing;
My spirit flew in feathers then,
That is so heavy now,
And summer pools could hardly cool,
The fever on my brow!

I remember, I remember,
The fir-trees dark and high;
I used to think their slender tops,
Were close against the sky:
It was a childish ignorance,
But now it's little joy,
To know I'm further off from the heaven,
Than when I was a boy.

Unit 9
In-flight Entertainment

Part I   Pre-listening

Tongue Twister

Coffee Pot

All I want is a proper cup of coffee made in a proper copper coffee pot, you can believe it or not, but I just want a cup of coffee in a proper coffee pot.

Tin coffee pots or iron coffee pots are of no use to me.

If I can't have a proper cup of coffee in a proper copper coffee pot, I'll have a cup of tea!

Pronunciation

I. Directions: You'll hear one word read from each group. Listen carefully and tick out the word you hear.

1. A. head   B. had   C. said   D. sad
2. A. hut   B. heart   C. cart   D. cat
3. A. full   B. pull   C. pool   D. pour
4. A. spots   B. shot   C. short   D. sports
5. A. isle   B. ale   C. oil   D. aisle
6. A. fail   B. foil   C. file   D. feel
7. A. loud   B. load   C. out   D. loot
8. A. cheers   B. sheer   C. chairs   D. share
9. A. cold   B. gold   C. coat   D. goat
10. A. pack   B. peg   C. bag   D. back

II. Assimilation

Directions: Listen carefully and repeat.

Assimilation is a phonological process in which two sounds that are different become more alike.

In connected speech, under the influence of the neighbors, sounds are replaced by another sound. Sometimes two neighboring sounds influence each other and are replaced by a third sound which is different from both the original sounds.

◎ light (p) blue
◎ that (p) mall
◎ get them [gettem]
◎ read these [ri:ddi:z]

Think and try to find out some more words like this.

Part II Listening In

Responses

You will hear five sentences. Listen carefully and select the best response to the question or statement.

1. A. I think so.
   B. Sure. Let me show you.
   C. OK. I will get you another one.

2. A. Yes, please.
   B. Of course. Here you are.
   C. You can press this button and select the channel you like.

3. A. Sorry, I don't know.
   B. Yes. We have magazines.
   C. Here you are.

4. A. The fourth one.

   B. Yes. There are several kinds of music.

   C. Yes. It's very nice.

5. A. What newspaper do you have?

   B. Thank you. I will.

   C. I see. Let me try.

Dialogue: Supplementary Reading Material

Word Study

supplementary: added to complete or make up a deficiency

material: the tangible substance that goes into the makeup of a physical object

suppose: expect, believe, or suppose

couple: a small indefinite number

pack: a convenient package or parcel

contain: include or contain; have as a component

crayon: writing implement consisting of a colored stick of composition wax used for writing and drawing

animated: having life or vigor or spirit

Listen to the following dialogue and choose the proper answer to the question.

1. At first, the passenger would like to have a copy of _____ to read.

   A. Washington Post.

   B. China Daily.

   C. The New York Times.

   D. CAAC In-Flight Magazine.

2. How old is the passenger's child?

   A. Five.

   B. Fifteen.

   C. Four.

   D. Fourteen.

3. A child pack doesn't contain _____.

   A. animated movies

   B. crayons

   C. fruits

   D. story-books

Unit 9 In-flight Entertainment

Dialogue: How to Use the Headsets?

Word Study

jack: an electrical device consisting of a connector socket designed for the insertion of a plug
press: exert pressure or force to or upon
button: an electrical switch operated by pressing
select: pick out, select, or choose from a number of alternatives
channel: a television station and its programs
opera: a drama set to music; consists of singing with orchestral accompaniment and an orchestral overture and interludes

Listen to the dialogue and fill in the missing words.

Passenger: Excuse me, Miss. 1._____?

Flight attendant: Yes, of course. What can I do for you?

Passenger: I don't know how to use the headsets. Will you tell me how to use them?

Flight attendant: OK. Let me 2._____ you how to use the headsets. First, put the 3._____ into your ears. Then, put the jack into this 4._____ at your 5._____. And last, press the button and select the channel you like.

Passenger: Can you help me 6._____ it? I want to listen to music.

Flight attendant: Certainly, there is rock music, 7._____ music, opera and so on. 8._____?

Passenger: I prefer rock music. I'm 9._____ about it. I often listen to my iPod while running.

Flight attendant: OK. Please press the button to select the 1st channel. I hope you will enjoy yourself.

Passenger: 10._____. Thank you very much.

Flight attendant: You're welcome.

Part III Listening and Understanding

09-3

Dialogue: Lift the Screen up

Word Study

correspond: be compatible, similar or consistent; coincide in their characteristics
assistance: the activity of contributing to the fulfillment of a need or furtherance of an effort

or purpose

lift: the act of raising something

screen: display on the surface of the large end of a cathode-ray tube on which is electronically created

slide: move obliquely or sideways, usually in an uncontrolled manner

cover: a covering that serves to conceal or shelter something

backward: at or to or toward the back or rear

unit: any division of quantity accepted as a standard of measurement or exchange

release: grant freedom to; free from confinement

suit: be agreeable or acceptable

switch: control consisting of a mechanical or electrical or electronic device for making or breaking or changing the connections in a circuit

considerate: showing concern for the rights and feelings of others

recommend: express a good opinion of

I. Listen to the dialogue and try to tell whether the following statements are true or not.

1. The flight attendant told the passenger that the music is the most beautiful language in the world. (   )

2. The passenger asked for another pair of headsets to bring them home. (   )

3. The passenger doesn't want to watch a movie. (   )

4. The passenger doesn't know how to lift the screen up. (   )

5. There is an interesting movie on channel four. (   )

II. Listen to the dialogue again and fill in the missing words.

A. The announcement

Ladies and gentlemen, now we will be 1._____ programs such as film, music and others. We hope you will enjoy them. Please use the 2._____ in the seat pocket in front of you. 3._____ which channel 4._____ with the programs that you wish to watch. You may ask your cabin attendants for 5._____ Thank you!

B. How to lift the screen up?

Let me show you. First open the 6._____, press this 7._____ and you can lift it up. After that you 8._____ this cover backwards so you can see the TV unit, then you just press it to 9._____ it. Now you can turn it to suit you and press this 10._____ on the arm.

Unit 9 In-flight Entertainment

Passage: The Entertainment System

> **Word Study**
>
> transmits: broadcast over the airwaves, as in radio or television
>
> comprises: include or contain; have as a component
>
> reproducers: an audio system that can reproduce and amplify signals to produce sound
>
> volume: the magnitude of sound
>
> designed: planned or created in an artistic or skilled manner
>
> delivered: bring to a destination, make a delivery
>
> comedy: light and humorous drama with a happy ending
>
> cartoons: a film made by photographing a series of cartoon drawings to give the illusion of movement when projected in rapid sequence
>
> variety: a collection containing a variety of sorts of things

I. Listen to the passage and try to tell whether the following statements are true or not.

1. The entertainment system provides the passengers with varied interesting video and audio programs during the flight. (   )

2. The passengers choose the program they want to listen to or watch by pressing the call button. (   )

3. A variety of music tracks are available in some flights, such as classical music, current popular hits, rock and roll, jazz, light music and opera. (   )

4. Before the program, the captain should distribute the headsets to each of the passengers. (   )

5. During the programs, the cabin attendants walk along the cabin aisle as usual, at least once every ten minutes. (   )

II. Listen carefully to the following passage again and choose the proper answers to the question.

1. The passenger can listen to the audio programs through the headsets connected to _____.

   A. the passenger audio reproducers

   B. the passenger channel push-buttons

   C. the passenger control units

   D. The passenger screen

2. The passenger control unit is installed on the _____ of each seat.

   A. armrest   B. back   C. top   D. channel

3. The passenger can adjust the volume by _____.

    A. pushing the upper or the lower volume push-buttons.

    B. pushing the upper or the lower channel push-buttons.

    C. pushing the upper or the lower audio push-buttons.

    D. pushing the upper or the lower video push-buttons.

4. The screen is either _____ or in the armrest.

    A. on the tray table in front of each passenger

    B. on the window shade in front of each passenger

    C. near the reading light in front of each passenger

    D. on the seat back in front of each passenger

5. At the beginning of the flight, the cabin attendants may be called upon to assist passengers, except _____.

    A. showing the operation of the headsets

    B. replacing faulty headset equipment

    C. singing a great song

    D. locating the proper channels

III. Listen to the passage again and fill in the missing words.

1. Each of the audio _____ gives a number of different music programs and the passenger control unit is _____ on the armrest of each seat.

2. Among these channels are _____ films such as drama, _____, comedy, romance, thriller, _____ and many video programs such as _____, cartoons and sports.

3. On many airplanes, _____ in first and business class cabins, the video programs can be watched on a small screen that is _____ to each seat.

4. The passengers can open the _____, take the headsets out, put it on and _____ it into the passenger control unit on the armrest.

Passage: Notting Hill

> **Word Study**
>
> actress: a female actor
>
> unattractive: lacking beauty or charm
>
> clerk: an employee who performs clerical work
>
> district: a region marked off for administrative or other purposes
>
> eccentric: a person with an unusual or odd personality
>
> polite: showing regard for others in manners, speech, behavior, etc.
>
> logically: according to logical reasoning

harmless: not causing or capable of causing harm
bloom: produce or yield flowers

Listen to the passage and fill in the missing words.

Can a beautiful and 1._____ famous American actress find happiness with an 2._____ and unattractive man, a British bookstore clerk? Yes, she can—3._____ for a while in Notting Hill. William Thacker is a 4._____ at a shop in the Notting Hill district in West London, who 5._____ a house with an eccentric Welsh friend, Spike. One day, William is minding the store when he sees Anna Scott, a lovely and 6._____ actress from the United States who is in London working on a film.

She buys a book from William, and she is polite and 7._____. Their relationship would logically end there, if William didn't run out a few minutes later and buy some juice. When quickly going back to the shop, he rans across Anna on the street, 8._____ juice all over her blouse. Since he lives nearby, William politely offers to let her stop by his house to 9._____; since William seems harmless enough, Anna agrees. When Anna has to stop back to pick up a bag she left at William's house, they kiss—just in time for Spike to show up. A 10._____ slowly blooms as his friends and family wonder what he's doing dating a movie star. What will happen to them?

Part IV   Listening and Enjoying

Cultural Perspective: Peking Opera

Word Study

extremely: to a high degree or extent; favorably or with much respect
dynasty: a sequence of powerful leaders in the same family
treasures: art highly prized for its beauty or perfection
respected: receiving deferential regard
origin: the place where something begins, where it springs into being
melody: a succession of notes forming a distinctive sequence
character: an actor's portrayal of someone in a play
opposite: characterized by opposite extremes; completely opposed
chief: a person who exercises control over workers

> masculine: a gender that refers chiefly (but not exclusively) to males or to objects classified as male
>
> contrast: the opposition or dissimilarity of things that are compared
>
> cosmetic: a toiletry designed to beautify the body
>
> figure: the impression produced by a person

Listen carefully to the following passage and try to find out the proper answers.

1. Peking opera is a kind of Chinese opera which arose in the _____ century.
   A. mid-18th   B. mid-19th   C. mid-20th   D. mid-21st

2. Beijing and _____ are respected as the base cities of Peking opera in the north.
   A. Tianjin   B. Shanghai   C. Hunan   D. Anhui

3. There are _____ main roles in Peking Opera.
   A. Two   B. Three   C. Four   D. Five

4. _____, which means "morning" or "masculine", is contrary to the feminine nature of the characters.
   A. Sheng   B. Dan   C. Jing   D. Chou

5. Which of the following statements is not true?
   A. Beijing opera got its two main melodies, Xipi and Erhuang, from Anhui and Hubei operas.
   B. It is said that the name of the main roles were chosen to have same meanings to their Chinese characters.
   C. Chou in Chinese sometimes represents the animal "ox", which, in some senses, is slow and silent.
   D. When it comes to types of facial makeup in Beijing opera, it is a national cosmetic with special feature.

Friends: The One with the Proposal

[Scene: The Hallway, Chandler is running up the stairs and towards his apartment, but Joey is taking out the garbage at the same time and stops him in the hall.]

Joey: Dude!

Chandler: I can't talk to you now, I gotta find Monica!

Joey: She's gone.

Chandler: What?

Joey: She's gone. She had a bag and she left.

Chandler: What are you talking about?

Joey: She was all crying. She-she said you guys want different things, and that and that she needed time to think.

Chandler: Well why didn't you stop her?! Why didn't you just tell her it was a plan?!

Joey: I-I did! I told her everything, Chandler! But she wouldn't believe me.

Chandler: Well where… Where did she go?

Joey: To her parent's I think and she said you shouldn't call her. But if I were you I would.

Chandler: I can't believe I ruined this.

Joey: I am so sorry man.

(He walks dejectedly into his apartment to find it lit with about a thousand candles and Monica standing in the living room.)

Monica: You wanted it to be a surprise.

(He turns to look at Joey who smiles slyly and closes the door leaving them alone.)

Chandler: Oh my God.

(Monica gets down on one knee.)

Monica: Chandler… In all my life… I never thought I would be so lucky. (Starting to cry.) As to…fall in love with my best…my best… There's a reason why girls don't do this!

Chandler: Okay! (He joins her on one knee) Okay! Okay! Oh God, I thought… (Starting to cry, pauses) Wait a minute, I-I can do this. (Pause) I thought that it mattered what I said or where I said it. Then I realized the only thing that matters is that you, (Pause) you make me happier than I ever thought I could be. (Starting to cry again.) And if you'll let me, I will spend the rest of my life trying to make you feel the same way. (Pause as he gets out the ring.) Monica, will you marry me?

Monica: Yes.

(The crowd goes wild as he puts the ring on her finger. They hug and kiss this time as an engaged couple.)

Monica: I knew you were likely to take a wife!

(They hug again.)

Joey: (yelling through the door) Can we come it yet?! We're dying out here!

Monica: Come in! Come in! (Joey, Rachel, and Phoebe burst through the door.) We're engaged!!!

(Everyone screams and has a group hug.)

Rachel: Oh, this is the least jealous I've ever been!

Phoebe: Oh no wait no, this is wrong! Ross isn't here!

Monica: Oh…

Rachel: Oh hell, he's done this three times! He knows what its about!

Joey: Yeah!

(They all hug again.)

Unit 10
Duty-free Sales

Unit 10　Duty-free Sales

Part I　Pre-listening

10-1

Idioms

Fill in the blanks and then try to find out their meanings.

1. French _____
2. Irish _____
3. Dutch _____
4. Dutch _____
5. _____ gift

Pronunciation

Contracted Forms

> It's quite common to use contracted forms in English, in both formal and informal situations. They help to connect the sentence and adjust the rhythm and intonation, which make the whole sentence fluent and native.

I. Listen to the following dialogue and underline the contracted words.

Susan: Have you been to Switzerland?

Jim: No, I haven't. But I plan to visit there next year.

Susan: Well, it's a really picturesque country: wonderful landscape, cultural diversity, global warming, and stunning outdoors.

Jim: Yes, that's why it's called world garden. My wife and I like traveling very much. And she's working on the schedule in detail.

Susan: There're so many things to do and to explore there. You'll love it definitely.

Jim: That'll be great! I can't wait to go.

II. Think and try to find out some other contracted forms.

Abbreviation

> Abbreviation is the short form of a word or a phrase, made by leaving out some of the letters or by using only the first letter of each word.

I. Write down the full name of these abbreviation words according to what you hear.

1. IATA（国际航空运输协会）
   _____

2. AC（中国国际航空公司）
   _____

3. ATC（空中管制）
   _____

4. UNESCO（联合国教科文组织）
   _____

5. ICAO（国际民航协会）
   _____

6. AUX（辅助设备）
   _____

II. Listen and write down the abbreviations.

1. _____
2. _____
3. _____
4. _____
5. _____
6. _____

Part II   Listening In

Responses

You will hear five sentences. Listen carefully and select the best response to the question or statement.

1. A. Yes, I think so.
   B. I'd choose the smaller one.
   C. I like purple better.

Unit 10　Duty-free Sales

2. A. Sure, you can.
   B. Yes, you can have some apples.
   C. It's behind the table.
3. A. No, there's no parking space.
   B. Either will be fine.
   C. It's not allowed.
4. A. Yes, here is your change.
   B. Sorry, I'm afraid not.
   C. Yes, it's not too far.
5. A. I can help you.
   B. No, it's not working.
   C. Yes, I'm interested in it.

Duty-free Announcement on Board

> ### Word Study
> frequent flyer: someone who often travels by plane, especially with the same airline
> bargain: try to persuade someone to give you a better price or make an agreement that suits you better
> excellent: extremely good or of very high quality

Listen to the announcement and fill in the missing words.

Ladies and gentlemen, the duty-free sales will begin 1._____. Please prepare your 2._____ of purchases. Check the Shopping on Board magazine in your seat 3._____. All prices are in 4._____ and in US dollars, and you can pay by cash or by using a credit card. We accept most major credit cards. Frequent flyers win 5._____ on all sales on board. There are some 6._____ bargains and there are several items specially designed for our airline.

Dialogue: Price for Items

Listen and tick the price you hear for each item.

> ### Word Study
> titanium: a strong, light, and very expensive metal
> zloty: the standard unit of money in Poland
> dirhams: the standard unit of money in Dubai

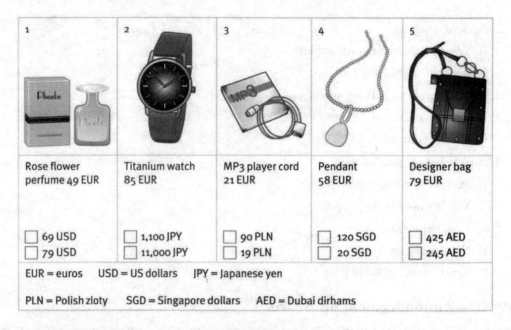

Dialogue: Souvenirs and Gifts on Board

> **Word Study**
>
> alcohol: intoxicating drinks containing alcohol
>
> delightful: giving great enjoyment and pleasure, especially by being pleasant, good to look at, or amusing
>
> classic: with all the features you would expect to find; very typical

Listen to the following dialogue and choose the proper answer to the question.

1. What does the passenger want to buy for his daughter?

    A. a classic perfume   B. a cheap perfume

    C. a delightful perfume   D. a very best perfume

2. How much does he pay for his daughter's present?

    A. 100USD   B. 65USD

    C. 41USD   D. 72USD

3. What else does the passenger buy?

    A. The very best perfume

    B. The airline's specially designed model

    C. bright colored scarves

    D. the pure silk scarves

4. How does he pay for his purchase?

    A. Master card   B. Frequent flyers miles

    C. Cash   D. Union pay

5. What does he need with his purchase?
   A. perfume
   B. scarves
   C. Frequent flyers card
   D. The receipt

Part III Listening and Understanding

Dialogue: In-flight Sales

> **Word Study**
>
> yen: the money unit in Japan
> resident: someone who lives or stays in a place such as a house or hotel

Listen to the following dialogue and choose the proper answer to the question.

1. What item is sold out according to the cabin attendant?
   A. Aircraft model
   B. Ferrero chocolate
   C. no item is sold out
   D. Godiva chocolate
2. How much of the Godiva chocolate in Japanese yen?
   A. 31   B. 40   C. 3100   D. 71
3. How much totally for all chocolates in USD?
   A. 111   B. 80   C. 40   D. 102
4. What's the requirement to buy the mail-order items?
   A. Must have the airline's member card
   B. Must make the pre-order
   C. Shall be the resident of Japan
   D. All above
5. Which are the final items that the passenger bought?
   A. 3 boxes of Godiva chocolate
   B. 2 boxes of Ferrero and 1 box of Godiva
   C. Aircraft model
   D. All of the items left.

Passage: Some Rules on In-flight Duty-free Purchase in CSA

> **Word Study**
>
> reservation: an arrangement made so that a place or product is kept for you
> allowance: an amount of something that it is acceptable of safe

restriction: a rule or system that limits or controls what you can do or what is allowed to happen

expenditure: the act of spending or using time, money, energy etc.

deficiency: a weakness or fault in something

accessory: something that you add or wear in order to make it attractive

warranty: a written promise that a company makes to replace or fix a product if it breaks or does not work properly

voucher: an official statement or receipt that is given to someone to prove that money has been paid or their accounts are correct

abuse: the use of something in a way that it should not be used

modification: a small change of something such as a design, plan or system

I. Listen to the following passage and choose the proper answer to the question.

1. Passengers traveling abroad can pre-order duty-free goods in the following ways except _____.

    A. By filling out a personal information form

    B. By making a phone call

    C. By visiting online stores

    D. By following the wechat

2. Which of the following statements is True about the duty-free allowances?

    A. Travelers can buy duty-free goods as much as they can.

    B. Duty-free allowances apply to the country where you buy the products.

    C. Each country has its own rules and restrictions on duty-free allowances.

    D. You'd better travel around the country before you buy .

3. Which of the following statements is not mentioned in the passage?

    A. Credit cards are acceptable to pay for the duty-free goods.

    B. All products sold in flight are marked in CNY.

    C. Each credit card can be used once only in each purchase.

    D. There is the expenditure limit to each person.

4. What would you do in case there is a quality problem with your duty-free product?

    A. Ask flight steward for help.

    B. Require a refund.

    C. Open and use it.

    D. Ask for a replacement.

5. What do you need to require for replacing faulty products?

    A. Packaging and manual.

    B. Accessories and gifts.

C. Warranty and shopping vouchers.

D. All of the above.

II. Listen to the following passage again and try to tell whether the following statements are true or not.

1. Passengers are permitted to buy duty-free products in either international or domestic flight. (   )

2. Passengers can pre-order the duty-free products by visiting online store at any time. (   )

3. When traveling abroad, there is no limit or restriction on what you buy. (   )

4. Only RMB and credit cards are acceptable to pay for duty-free goods. (   )

5. Passengers need to ask for a replacement for the faulty products within a month since purchase. (   )

6. Replacing goods requires shopping vouchers only. (   )

Part IV   Listening and Enjoying

Star Alliance

I. Listen to the following passage and choose the proper answer to the question.

1. How many member airlines are there in Star Alliance?

   A. 197   B. 28

   C. 1300   D. 192

2. Which country is not the original member of Star Alliance?

   A. Air China   B. Lufthansa

   C. United Airlines   D. Air Canada

3. What benefits can silver passengers have in Star Alliance?

   A. Desired connection

   B. Appropriate ground service

   C. Priority boarding

   D. All of the above

4. Which of the following statements is NOT mentioned?

   A. Star Alliance is based in Germany.

   B. Its slogan is The Way the Earth Connects.

   C. Star Alliance takes more market share than other alliances.

   D. Air China is a member of "Move Under One Roof" program.

5. What does the word "co-locate" mean here?
   A. Share the same airport
   B. Two airports
   C. Another location
   D. Find a new location

Yoga

II. Listen to the following passage and fill in the missing words.

Yoga was _____ in India thousands of years ago. The word "Yoga" means to "yoke" or "unite". Patanjal is often considered the father of yoga and his Yoga-Sutras still strongly influence most styles of modern yoga.

It is a _____ misconception that yoga requires people to twist themselves into pretzels or stand on their heads. Not only do you not have to be _____ to practise yoga, you also don't need to be young or fit or even ambulatory. In fact, the only requirement for practising yoga is the ability to breathe or meditate.

Regular stretching exercises on strength and patience can improve cardio-pulmonary _____ and coordinate the organism effectively. Yogis try to control themselves by activating potential in their body and stimulating the body's own _____ healing process.

Yoga now has many different _____ or styles, all emphasizing the many different aspects of the practice. The top aim is to get spiritual purification through creating a sense of _____ in the body and mind.

It is quite popular now as a _____ of exercise and relaxation to shape the body and _____ the stress of modern living. In recent years, an increasing number of scientific studies have measured yoga's effectiveness as a treatment for various ailments, including improving blood pressure, relieving pain, enhancing sleep and boosting _____.

Unit 11
Service for Special Passengers

Part I   Pre-listening

Tongue Twisters

Try to read out two or three of the following tongue twisters fluently. Pay attention to your pronunciation.

1. Peter Piper picked a peck of pickled peppers.
   A peck of pickled peppers Peter Piper picked.
   If Peter Piper picked a peck of pickled peppers,
   Where's the peck of pickled peppers Peter Piper picked?
2. The thirty-three thieves thought that they thrilled the throne throughout Thursday.
3. Denise sees the fleece,
   Denise sees the fleas.
   At least Denise could sneeze
   and feed and freeze the fleas.
4. How many boards
   Could the Mongols hoard
   If the Mongol hordes got bored?
5. Send toast to ten tense stout saints' ten tall tents.
6. I saw Susie sitting in a shoe shine shop.
   Where she sits she shines, and where she shines she sits.
7. How can a clam cram in a clean cream can?

Pronunciation

Directions: You'll hear a passage about intonation. Check your understanding of the passage and choose the best answer.

1. Language can tell us _____.
   A. How a speaker feels about what he is saying
   B. How a speaker feels at the moment he is speaking
   C. Both of the above
2. If your intonation patterns are not standard, _____.
   A. everyone will understand you
   B. your meaning will probably not be clear
   C. neither of the above
3. What is usually stressed in a sentence?
   A. Every word   B. Nouns   C. Pronouns

4. After the nouns have been introduced and we begin using pronouns, which words are usually stressed?

　　A. Verbs　　　　　　B. Pronouns　　　　　C. Adjectives

Intonation

Directions: Listen and try to read the following sentences. Pay attention to the intonation.

> Intonation describes how the voice rises and falls in speech. The three main patterns of intonation in English are: falling intonation, rising intonation and fall-rise intonation.

Falling Intonation

Falling intonation describes how the voice falls on the final stressed syllable of a phrase or a group of words. A falling intonation is very common in **Wh-** questions.

◎ Where's the nearest p↘ost-office?

◎ What time does the film f↘inish?

We also use falling intonation when we say something definite, or when we want to be very clear about something.

◎ I think we are completely l↘ost.

◎ OK, here's the magaz↘ine you wanted.

Rising Intonation

Rising intonation describes how the voice rises at the end of a sentence. Rising intonation is common in yes-no questions.

◎ I hear the Health Centre is expanding. So, is that the new d↗octor?

◎ Are you th↗irsty?

Fall-rise Intonation

Fall-rise intonation describes how the voice falls and then rises. We use fall-rise intonation at the end of statements when we want to say that we are not sure, or when we may have more to add.

◎ I do↘n't support any football team at the m↘om↗ent. (but I may change my mind in the future).

◎ It rained every day in the firs↘t w↗eek. (but things improved after that).

We use fall-rise intonation with questions, especially when we request information or invite somebody to do or to have something. The intonation pattern makes the questions sound more polite.

◎ Is this your cam↘er↗a?

◎ Would you like another co↘ff↗ee?

Think and try to read out the following announcements. Pay attention to your intonation.

1. There are eight (ten) emergency exits / located at the forward↗, rear↗ and middle↘.

2. We would ask you to ensure that (the window shade is open) ↗, (your seatbelt fastened) ↗, (your tray table stowed) ↗ and (your seatback brought to the upright position) ↘.

Part II Listening In

Responses

You will hear five sentences. Listen carefully and select the best response to each question or statement.

1. A. She is ten years old.
   B. How old is she?
   C. Yes. There are two.

2. A. Have a nice trip.
   B. Please fill in this form.
   C. I don't know.

3. A. Sorry, I won't.
   B. Thank you.
   C. It doesn't matter.

4. A. It's a boy.
   B. Five months.
   C. I'm not comfortable.

5. A. It's Tuesday.
   B. It's April the 20th.
   C. It's a good day.

Dialogue: Service for Special Passengers

Linda works as a flight attendant in the Sky Airlines. Today her flight is from Tokyo to Hong Kong. There are several special passengers in today's flight. Listen carefully and fill in the missing information and preference, please.

> **Word Study**
>
> nickname: n. A nickname is an informal name for someone or something
> unaccompanied : without accompaniment or companions
> pregnant: carrying developing offspring within the body or being about to produce new life
> blind: adj. unable to see

n. people who have severe visual impairments, considered as a group

infant: a very young child (birth to 1 year) who has not yet begun to walk or talk

vacant: without an occupant or incumbent

bassinet: A bassinet is a small bed for a baby that is like a basket

vomit: If you vomit, food and drink comes back up from your stomach and out through your mouth.

Name	Special Passenger	Matters Need Attention
Tomas Anderson	unaccompanied _____	• take him to his _____ • help him fasten his _____ • keeping his _____ and return ticket
Ms. Smith	pregnant	• She has been pregnant about _____ weeks. • help adjust the _____ and air vent • an _____ is in the seat pocket • provide with a _____ and water
Richard Merman	blind passenger	• help with his _____ • take him to his seat if he likes • introduce the meal: the tray set is like _____
Dianna	passenger with a _____	• there is no _____ on board • try to find some _____ seat • lift up the _____ for the baby to lie down • help to fasten the _____ seatbelt

Dialogue: Check-in for Special Passengers

Word Study

disable: make unable to perform a certain action

assistance: the activity of contributing to the fulfillment of a need or furtherance of an effort or purpose

exceptions clause: non-responsibility; A clause is a section of a legal document

wheelchair: a movable chair mounted on large wheels; for invalids or those who cannot walk

I. Listen to the following dialogue and choose the proper answer to the question.

1. How many special passengers are mentioned in this dialogue?
   A. One   B. Two   C. Three   D. Four

2. How many bags are the gentleman checking in?
   A. Only one piece of baggage.   B. Two pieces of baggage.
   C. Three pieces of baggage.   D. He's not checking any.

3. How old is the child?

  A. 9 years old   B. 10 years old

  C. 11 years old   D. 12 years old

4. What information is not mentioned in the form of disabled passenger?

  A. Personal information   B. Situation of an illness

  C. Where he is traveling to   D. Exceptions clause

5. What information is not mentioned in the form of Unaccompanied Children?

  A. Telephone number   B. Destination

  C. Special needs   D. Address

II. Listen to the dialogue again and try to tell whether the following statements are true or not.

1. The lady here is checking in for her husband. ( )

2. The lady has to read the exceptions clause carefully and sign. ( )

3. The disabled gentleman needn't check in his wheelchair. ( )

4. The disabled gentleman's seat is in the last row. ( )

5. If you check in for an unaccompanied child, you will fill in a form. ( )

Dialogue: Passenger with an Infant

Word Study

stroller: A stroller is a small chair on wheels, in which a baby or small child can sit and be wheeled around

scale: a set of levels

milk powder: dehydrated milk; dry milk

scoop: to remove something out of a container with things like a spoon

Listen carefully to the following interview and try to find out the proper answers.

1. Could the passenger's stroller be put in the cabin?

  A. Yes.   B. No.

  C. Yes, but she need to go through the security check.   D. Not mentioned.

2. Where is the passenger's destination?

  A. Peking.   B. New York.

  C. San Francisco.   D. Hong Kong.

3. Who will pick up the stroller in advance and bring it at the cabin door?

  A. The flight attendant.   B. The captain.

  C. The ground staff.   D. The passenger's husband.

4. How many spoons of milk powder does the passenger need for her daughter?

   A. Three.   B. Five.
   C. Six.   D. Eight.

5. Why is the baby crying?

   A. She may feel the uncomfortable pressure.
   B. She is ill.
   C. She's hungry.
   D. She needs her mother.

Part III Listening and Understanding

Dialogue: Upgrading

> **Word Study**
>
> upgrade: If you upgrade or are upgraded, you change something such as your plane ticket or your hotel room to one that is more expensive

Number the sentences in the correct order according to the dialogue.

○ Our first class is fully booked today.
○ That's okay. Thank you.
○ We are unable to offer you such a seat today.
○ There are only front window seats now.
○ Is there anything I can do for you?
○ The middle seat is too narrow and it makes me uncomfortable.
○ May I have an upgrade?

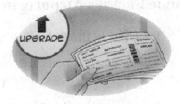

Passage: Assistance for Incapacitated Passengers

> **Word Study**
>
> incapacitated: lacking in or deprived of strength or power
> physical: Physical qualities, actions, or things are connected with a person's body, rather than with their mind
> mental: involving the mind or an intellectual process

embark: go on board

permanent: lasts forever

surgery: medical treatment in which someone's body is cut open so that a doctor can repair, remove, or replace a diseased or damaged part

Listen to the passage and fill in the missing words.

Incapacitated passengers are those who, because of their medical, _____ or mental condition, require individual attention which is not normally provided to other passengers. This attention may be required on _____, disembarking, in-flight, in an _____ or during ground handling.

Some incapacitated passengers may have _____ but stable disabilities, such as arthritis, deafness, _____, or paralysis of all or part of the body. Others may have temporary disabilities such as recent _____, broken limbs, or recent illness which requires them to be on a stretcher or in a _____.

Not all incapacitated passengers require medical _____ before being accepted for travel. However, passengers with the following incapacities or disabilities must be _____ medical clearance by our Medical Services Department before being accepted for travel.

If you have enquiries _____ the assistance provided for specific conditions, please call our customer care center at 503 4798 5000.

Part IV   Listening and Enjoying

Some Famous Airports in the World

I. Listen to the following passage and choose the proper answer to the question.

1. How many airports are mentioned in the passage?

   A. 2   B. 3   C. 4   D. 5

2. Where is Heathrow International Airport?

   A. The United States.   B. The United Kingdom.

   C. Japan.   D. Saudi Arabia.

3. Which airport is the third-busiest airport in the world by passenger traffic?

   A. Heathrow International Airport.

   B. Beijing Capital International Airport.

   C. Incheon International Airport.

   D. Dubai International Airport.

4. Which airport operates as a hub for cargo traffic and international civilian air

transportation in East Asia?

　　A. Heathrow International Airport.

　　B. Beijing Capital International Airport.

　　C. Incheon International Airport.

　　D. Dubai International Airport.

5. Beijing Airport is not a hub for _____.

　　A. Air China　　　　　　　　　　B. China Southern Airlines

　　C. Shandong Airlines　　　　　　D. Xiamen Airlines

II. Enjoy the song and complete the missing lyrics.

Winter in My Heart

Winter has come
farewell to the sun
it's getting colder every _____ day

you are not here
can't stand you're not near
I'll wait for you forever and I pray
my _____ makes me believe that you're with me

I have winter in my heart
cause I miss you more than _____ can say
when nights are long and _____ without you

I have winter in my heart
count the hours every single day
that _____ time is too sad to be true
got winter in my heart

snow _____ down
and you're not around
I'm all alone in that white _____
taking a walk
there's no one to _____
we used to be _____ hand in hand
my fantasy makes me believe that you're with me

I have winter in my heart
cause I miss you more than words can say
when nights are long and lonely without you
I have winter in my heart
_____ the hours every single day
that lonesome time is too sad to be true
got winter in my heart

Unit 12
Emergency Situations

Part I   Pre-listening

Slangs

Complete the following sentences and then try to find out the meanings of the slangs about "fish".

1. Mr. Smith looks like a _____ fish.

2. I can't believe it! His only daughter was hurt in an _____ and he didn't go to the hospital just because he had other fish to _____——a million-dollar deal he was closing.

3. Never _____ to teach fish to swim.

4. In her hometown, she was a big fish in a small _____, but after then moved to New York, she was just only one among many millions.

5. It's like _____ fish in a barrel.

Pronunciation

Sense groups

It's depressing to listen to or read a long sentence without pausing. However, we cannot pause wherever we want. We need to make sense of the sentence by breaking it into meaningful groups. It's hardly noticeable but enough to make the sentence more fluent and understandable.

I. Read the following paragraph and mark the sense groups with "/".

College students can get an assistance from the government when they cannot afford their tuition fee. Eligible students can be granted with an unequal amounts including living cost according to their family status. Otherwise, students may choose to apply to the Students Loans Company for a student loan with low interest rate. Loans are supposed to be repaid after they graduate and get a job.

II. Answer the questions according to what you hear.

1. Who?   _____

2. Where?   _____

3. What?   _____

4. How? _____
5. How long? _____
6. Why? _____
7. How much? _____
8. How often? _____
9. When? _____
10. Whom? _____

Part II   Listening In

12-2

Responses

You will hear five sentences. Listen carefully and select the best response to each question or statement.

1. A. Yes, my pleasure.
   B. That won't help.
   C. It's near the airport.

2. A. Yes, the plane is delayed.
   B. I'm playing the piano.
   C. It's the storm.

3. A. It takes about 5 hours.
   B. I don't like a morning flight.
   C. Let me ask the stuff here.

4. A. Neither, please.
   B. Help yourself, please.
   C. The ice cream is melted.

5. A. Don't push the button.
   B. Ask the Purser to make sure.
   C. Yes, it's alright.

Dialogues: Medical Problems

> **Word Study**
>
> plaster: a piece of thin material to cover skin cuts and other small wounds
> bleed: to lose blood especially because of an injury

> tissue: a piece of soft thin paper used especially for blowing your nose on
> swallow: to make this kind of movement with your throat

Listen and match each conversation with a medical problem.

Conversations   Problems

Conversation 1   a. a nosebleed

Conversation 2   b. an earache

Conversation 3   c. a cut in the head

Announcement: Sudden Emergency Announcement

Try to fill in the missing words of the following sudden announcement from the purser. Then listen and check your answers.

Ladies and gentlemen, this is an 1._____. This is an emergency. 2._____ in your seats with your seat belts 3._____. Remain 4._____ and 5._____ these instructions. Pull down the oxygen mask. Pull down the oxygen mask. Put it 6._____ your nose and 7._____ immediately and breathe 8._____. Adjust the 9._____ to secure it. Do make sure your own mask is fitted properly 10._____ helping anyone else.

Dialogue: The Injured Passenger on Board

> **Word Study**
>
> dizzy: having or involving a sensation of spinning around and losing one's balance
> nasty: highly unpleasant, especially to the senses
> forehead: the part of the face above the eyebrows
> compress: a pad of absorbent material pressed onto part of the body to relieve inflammation or stop bleeding.

Listen carefully and choose the proper answer to the question.

1. Who is the injured passenger traveling with?

    A. With her husband   B. The man who just went back

    C. With a woman   D. Nobody

2. What happened to the injured passenger?

    A. She got a crash on her forehead when turbulence.

    B. She had a nasty bang on her head.

    C. She was fine without any bad feeling.

    D. She got a headache on board.

3. How did the cabin crew deal with the injured passenger?

    A. They didn't use the first aid kit.

Unit 12　Emergency Situations

　　B. Leila helped clean up the wound and put a dressing over it.
　　C. Leila got the passenger a glass of water.
　　D. They didn't take any action to deal with the wound, only asked the passenger's feeling.
　4. What did Leila want the injured passenger to do?
　　A. Take some medicine   B. Go to have a seat
　　C. compress against the forehead   D. Both B and C

Dialogue: Is there a Doctor on Board?

> **Word Study**
>
> unconscious: the part of the mind that is inaccessible to the conscious mind but that affects behavior and emotions
> defibrillator: an apparatus used to control heart fibrillation by application of an electric current to the chest wall or heart
> heart attack: a sudden and sometimes fatal occurrence of coronary thrombosis, typically resulting in the death of part of a heart muscle
> indigestion: pain or discomfort in the stomach associated with difficulty in digesting food
> collapsed: (of a person) fall down and become unconscious, typically through illness or injury
> diabetic: a person suffering from diabetes
> CPR: cardiopulmonary resuscitation
> pulse: a rhythmical throbbing of the arteries as blood is propelled through them, typically as felt in the wrists or neck
> shallow: of little depth

Listen to the dialogue and try to tell whether the following statements are true or not.
1. The sick passenger is unconscious. (　　)
2. The sick passenger is travelling alone. (　　)
3. The sick passenger is 73 years old. (　　)
4. Rani needs help from other passengers, so he ask them to stay around the sick passenger. (　　)
5. Rani wants to put the sick passenger in a seat. (　　)
6. The sick passenger had collapsed before. (　　)
7. Rani and Bill give the sick passenger oxygen. (　　)
8. Rani and Bill can deal with the situation themselves. (　　)
9. The sick passenger is on medication. (　　)
10. The sick passenger is in good health. (　　)
11. Sarah tells Anton, the purser, about the situation. (　　)
12. There isn't a doctor on board. (　　)

Part III Listening and Understanding

Dialogue: Emergency commands

> **Word Study**
>
> evacuation: the action of emptying the bowels or another bodily organ
> concise: giving a lot of information clearly and in a few words; brief but comprehensive
> motivate: raise levels of physiological or nervous activity in (the body or any biological system)
> brace: make (a structure) stronger or firmer with wood, iron, or other forms of support
> ditch: bring (an aircraft) down on water in an emergency
> release: allow or enable to escape from confinement; set free

Choose the emergency command to match the emergency situation according to what you hear.

Emergency Situations	Emergency Commands
1. Bracing commands, in an unanticipated emergency	A. Inflate your life vest! Step through! Turn. Go off the front of the wing!
2. Bracing commands, in an anticipated emergency command.	B. Grab ankles! Head Down! Stay low!
3. The Evacuation commands of the ditching situation to evacuate.	C. Brace!
	D. You two, stay at the bottom! Help people off!
4. In the emergency landing, command the first two able-bodied passengers evacuating.	E. Release seat belts! Get your life vest! Get up! Get out!
5. In the ditching situation, instruct passenger to go off the front of the wing.	

Announcement: Preparing for an Emergency Evacuation

> **Word Study**
>
> slide: a piece of equipment that has a steep slope to go down
> instruction: a statement telling someone what they must do
> procedure: the correct or normal way of doing something
> tear: to damage something by pulling it too hard or letting it touch something

I. Listen to the following dialogue and choose the proper answer to the question.

1. According to the captain's announcement, what will they use to evacuate from the

aircraft?

A. lift raft   B. escape routes   C. evacuation slide   D. oxygen masks

2. What does the purser not mention about the safety procedures?

A. safety card   B. life jackets   C. Emergency exits   D. flashing light

3. How many emergency exits are on the upper deck?

A. 2   B. 5   C. 8   D. 6

4. Which of the following statements is correct?

A. Passengers can evacuate with all personal belongings.

B. This emergency evacuation will be dangerous if passengers don't follow the commands.

C. The safety card in your overhead compartment shows details of your escape routes, oxygen masks and life jackets.

D. passengers must remain seated and follow instructions by captain.

II. Listen to the dialogue again and try to tell whether the following statements are true or not.

1. The reason that the captain decided to emergency landing was the abnormal aircraft altitude. (   )

2. Captain decided to land in the next 20 minutes at the nearest airport. (   )

3. The first command from the purser was the passengers must return to seat immediately and fasten seatbelt. (   )

4. Use the furthest exit to evacuate . (   )

5. It's forbidden to bring everything when evacuating. (   )

6. Passengers can evacuate with high-heeled shoes. (   )

7. When the seatbelt signs are switched off, passengers can run. (   )

Part IV   Listening and Enjoying

12-4

Passage: Film on Pilot's Heroic Story to Begin Shooting

Liu Chuanjian (left in second row), Sichuan Airlines' heroic pilot, posing for a photo with the film crew, including Zhang Hanyu (middle in second row), on board after he piloted a flight from Chengdu to Beijing on Nov 16. [Photo provided to chinadaily.com.cn]

Word Study

heroic: very brave

windshield: a window at the front of pilots' seat in the cockpit

hail: acclaim enthusiastically as being a specified thing

Number the sentences in the correct order according to the passage.

○ Liu Chuanjian, a Sichuan Airlines' captain.

○ Therefore, after successfully handling an emergency landing, the captain Liu and his heroic story will hit screens in China.

○ Popular actor Zhang Hanyu will feature in the movie to be directed by Liu Weiqiang. The film will start shooting in January and is expected to hit screens within 2019.

○ At that time, he was operating the Airbus A319 from Chongqing to Lhasa, Tibet.

○ Liu was honored with five million yuan ($730,000) prize and hailed the "hero captain of China's civil aviation".

○ A windshield suddenly broke at 32,000 feet above the ground and his co-pilot was sucked halfway out of the window and was saved by the seat belt.

○ In May 2018, he calmly landed a flight after a 20-minute struggle with the loss of cabin pressure

◎ Liu landed the plane safely with none of the passengers injured.

Culture Perspective: Tennis Tournaments

Choose the words you hear to fill in the blanks.

dressed	lake	tradition	courts	associates	qualified
originally	late	enforcing	considered	course	championship
tournaments	classified	Grand	originated	body	Membership
promoting	associations				

Court tennis is also known as royal tennis. It _____ in France during the Middle Ages. It is a tradition that players must be dressed in white sportswear. In 1884, Wimbledon inaugurated a women's _____.

There are four major tennis _____ in the world. Wimbledon is _____ as the oldest and the most important one. It is held in _____ June and early July every year. Unlike Wimbledon which is played on grass, the US Open, the French Open and the Australia Open are played on clay or hard _____. "Open" originally meant that any players can take part in the competition if they want. But now, only players with certain rank can be _____ for the competition. Among the four tournaments, the Us Open offers the most prize money.

Winning all four in the same year is called a grand slam. Don Budge was the first winner of the _____ Slam tournaments in 1938.

ITF (The International Tennis Federation) is the governing _____ of world tennis, wheelchair tennis, and beach tennis. It was founded in 1913 by twelve national _____ and as of 2016, is affiliated with 211 national tennis associations and six regional associations. The ITF's governance responsibilities include maintaining and _____ the rules of tennis, regulating international team competitions, _____ the game, and preserving the sport's integrity via anti-doping and anti-corruption programs.

Unit 13
Transfer Service

Unit 13 Transfer Service

Part I Pre-listening

13-1

Opposites

Try to write down the opposites of the following words.

1. light————————
2. major————————
3. coward————————
4. safe————————
5. deep————————
6. exit————————

Pronunciation

I. Write down the names of cities or countries you hear.

	Country	Capital	City	Language
1				
2				
3				
4				
5				
6				
7				
8				

II. Complete this part as well as you possibly can.

Schedule

Dr. Harrison is going to Rome on business. Please complete his timetable according to what you hear.

March			
21st	Tuesday	10:10 a.m.	Flight _____ to Paris
		18:30 p.m.	dinner with Mr. Morris
22nd	_____	9:30 a.m.	visit new factory
		12:10 p.m.	lunch with Ms. Albert
		14:30 p.m.	_____
____	Thursday	all day	attend the fair
24th	Friday	9:00 a.m.	_____
		15:50 p.m.	Flight 652 back

Part II Listening In

Responses

You will hear five sentences. Listen carefully and select the best response to the question or statement.

1. A. Ask the stewardess for it.
   B. Yes, there is a blanket.
   C. Don't forget to take it.
2. A. By air mail.
   B. Yes, it arrived on time.
   C. In 3 days or so.
3. A. Let me show you.
   B. Yes, I need your help.
   C. You can open another account.
4. A. It's good to me.
   B. No, it's not completed.
   C. I'm sorry to hear that. What can I help you with?
5. A. I plan to get there by air.
   B. You can board now.
   C. A non-stop flight.

Dialogue: My Luggage in Connecting Flight

Listen to the following dialogue and choose the proper answer to the question.

> **Word Study**
>
> immigration: the place at a port, airport, or international border where officials check the passports of people who wish to come into the country
> shuttle: an aircraft (train, bus, etc.) used for traveling back and forth
> relief: feel happy because something unpleasant has not happened or is no longer happening

1. Where does the man want to go?
   A. Home   B. Italy   C. Bangkok   D. California
2. What flight is the man traveling with?
   A. Bangkok airline   B. A partner
   C. A member airline of Star Alliance   D. Immigration officer

Unit 13 Transfer Service

3. Does the man have to check in again?
   A. Yes, he does.
   B. No, he doesn't.
   C. Yes, he has to check through the immigration.
   D. No, he doesn't have to be relief.
4. How can he get to the terminal?
   A. Walk on foot.   B. Take the bus.
   C. Take the shuttle train.   D. Take the subway.

Passage: Why Book Your Airport Transfer with Us?

Word Study

limousine: a big and comfortable car that people take to and from airport
inclusive: If a price is inclusive, it includes the cost of everything
cover: a guarantee from insurance company against injury, damage, etc.
voucher: a kind of ticket that can be used instead of money for a particular purpose
valid: If a ticket or other document is valid, it can be used legally or officially
redeem: to exchange the amount of money that it is worth
offset: If one thing is offset by another, the effect of the first thing is reduced by the second so that the situation remains the same
access: the right to enter a place
complimentary: free of charge

Listen to the following passage and fill in the missing words.

Conxxe is a worldwide transport service, offering you airport to city and 1)_____ transfers in over 21,000 destinations in over 150 countries around the world.

• Comfortable transport from/to airports
   Wide range of safe & licensed 2)_____, including cars, shared shuttles & chauffeured limousines
• Outstanding value & quality service
• Fully inclusive 3)_____, no 4)_____ extras
• Pre-book online and avoid queues for a hassle free arrival
• 22,000+ positive independent customer 5)_____
• 24/7 service and support helpline, emergency cover gives peace of mind
• $20 6)_____ voucher is valid from now till September 30, 2020 to offset your 7)_____ shopping and dinning during your transit at our airport. The transit voucher can also be redeemed for one-time access to the Ambassador Lounge at 8)_____ 2 or 3 for

up to two hours; as well as selected spa and massage services at Spa Express in Terminal 2. The Ambassador 9)_____ provides shower facilities (including basic toiletries), 10)_____ refreshments, reading material and complimentary WiFi.

Dialogue: Free Singapore Bus Tour During Your Transit

Word Study

heritage: important qualities, traditions, or features that have been in a society for a long time and passed on from one generation to another

litter: If something is littered with things, it contains a lot of things in it

stark: very different from each other in a way that is very obvious

withstand: still be important or effective etc after a long time

icon: as an important symbol of a particular thing

panoramic: an impressive view of a wide area of land

esplanade: a wide road by the sea where people can walk for pleasure

brochure: a magazine or thin book with pictures giving information or advertising a product or service

I. Listen to the following dialogue and choose the proper answer to each question.

1. How long will the woman stay in Singapore?

    A. 2.5 hours	B. More than 5.5 hours

    C. Less than 5.5 hours	D. Two days

2. Which of the following statements about Heritage Tour is true?

    A. Heritage Tour is to visit modern skyscrapers.

    B. Heritage Tour is better than City Sights Tour.

    C. There are quiet a few of historical monuments.

    D. The woman doesn't like Heritage Tour.

3. Which of the following place is not included in City Sights Tour?

    A. Changi Airport	B. Singapore Flyer

    C. Marina Bay Sands	D. Gardens by the Bay

4. Which route is the woman recommended to choose?

    A. Heritage Tour	B. City Sights Tour

    C. Both	D. Neither

5. Which of the following is similar in meaning with the word "withstand"?

    A. To stand up	B. To be different

    C. To make a contrast	D. To go through

II. Listen to the following dialogue again and try to tell whether the following statements are true or not.

1. The woman plans to visit friends in Singapore. (   )
2. The city hall is newly built in the colonial district. (   )
3. The Merlion is a national symbol of Singapore. (   )
4. Two Tour routes take 2.5 hours long in all. (   )
5. City Sights Tour offers the night view of Singapore's famous icons along the Marina Bay. (   )

Part III   Listening and Understanding

13-3

Dialogue: Unaccompanied Minor Lounges For Connection

Listen to the following dialogue and choose the proper answer to each question.

> **Word Study**
>
> unaccompanied: someone who is unaccompanied has no one with them
> supervise: to be in charge of a group of people and be responsible for making sure they do their work properly

1. What kind of passengers does unaccompanied minor service apply to?
   A. National minorities   B. People working for companies
   C. Children without their parents   D. Children who travel alone
2. What documents do parents or guardians need to provide when checking-in?
   A. Child's birth certificate
   B. Parents' contact information
   C. Information of the adult meeting at destination
   D. All of the above.
3. Which of the following statements is not mentioned?
   A. Parents or guardians need to go through customs with their child.
   B. Parents or guardians need to provide their contact information.
   C. Her daughter is going to transfer at Dubai Airport.
   D. There are lounges for her daughter to rest during the connection.
4. What service is not included at the lounges for connection?
   A. A supervisor   B. An airport tour
   C. Video games   D. Drinks and snacks

5. What does the word "supervise" mean?

   A. To travel   B. To provide

   C. To be responsible for   D. To appreciate

Passage: A Transit Visa

Word Study

designate: to choose someone or something for a particular purpose

eligibility: someone who is eligible to do something is able or allowed to do it

criteria: a standard established to judge or decide something

schengen: an area of 26 European countries that have officially abolished all other types of boarder control at their mutual borders with a common visa policy

I. Listen to the following passage and then choose the proper answer to each question.

1. When is a transit visa used for?

   A. To enter another country   B. To leave another country

   C. To transfer through a country   D. To go through an airport

2. Which of the following statements is not true?

   A. An airport transit visa holder can stay in the country for no more than 48 hours.

   B. A visitor transit visa holder can stay in the country as long as they can.

   C. An airport transit visa holder can stay within the airport.

   D. A visitor transit visa permits holders to go outside of the airport.

3. Which of the following statements is not mentioned here?

   A. A transit visa is free of charge.

   B. The restrictions are different.

   C. Each country has its own criteria on a transit visa.

   D. A transit visa application needs photographs in Thailand.

4. What does the word "eligibility" mean here?

   A. Transit   B. Qualification

   C. Mobility   D. Flexibility

5. Which of the following statements is true?

   A. A Schengen transit visa is needed for a citizen of EEA.

   B. Australian government permits transit visa holders to stay longer than 72 hours.

   C. Chinese people need to apply for a transit visa with 2 application forms and 4 photographs.

   D. The regulations and standards are different from country to country.

II. Listen again and make a correct order of the following sentences.

1. When traveling through a Schengen country, you don't need to apply for a transit Schengen visa if you are a family member of a citizen of the European Union.

2. Usually there are two types of transit visas: airport transit visa and visitor transit visa.

3. When applying for a transit visa in Thailand, Chinese people need to submit 2 application forms and 2 photographs.

4. The restrictions or eligibility criteria are subject to change to certain conditions.

5. The latter one is granted to travelers who need to go out of the airport.

Part IV   Listening and Enjoying

Recruitment

Listen to the following advertisement and then choose the proper answer to the questions.

1. What position is wanted?
   A. Tennis player
   B. Chinese attendant
   C. Inflight interpreter
   D. Chief purser

2. What duty is not mentioned?
   A. To help crew with products and service
   B. To promote the communication between customers and cabin crew
   C. To provide customers' feedback to the chief purser
   D. To work independently

3. What qualifications are required for the position?
   A. Communication skills
   B. Good command of French and Mandarin
   C. University graduate
   D. All of the above

4. Which of the following statements is not true?
   A. The position is based in Guangzhou.
   B. The applicant needs to be a female at thirties.
   C. The applicant needs to know French culture.
   D. The candidate had better send the application before the mid-June.

5. What does the word "plus" mean here?
   A. advantage
   B. application
   C. requirement
   D. communication

Cultural Perspective: Iceland

Listen to the introduction to Iceland and fill in the missing words.

The Republic of Iceland is an island country in North Europe, and the Europe's second-largest island after Great Britain. One ____1____ of the country is covered with glaciers. The land is a bowl-like plateau surrounded with ____2____ and lava fields.

There are more than 100 ____3____ in Iceland, 40 to 50 of which are active ones. That is why Iceland is full of hot ____4____, beautiful colored rocks and other natural wonders. It's also known as A Country of Ice and Fire.

The ____5____ is Reykjavik, a port city and also the largest city. Iceland has the smallest population in Europe. Historically, its economy depends heavily on fishing and ____6____ supply. Legally, there is no standing army with a lightly armed Coast Guard. People here travel by road since there is no ____7____ railway, but a great number of roads are unpaved. Icelanders are among the world's healthiest people. The average life ____8____ is 81.8, the 4th highest in the world.

Despite a high ____9____ just outside the Arctic Circle, Iceland has a temperate climate in winter because of the Gulf Stream, about -2℃ in average. Visitors can experience ____10____ days in summer or play snow locomotive or cross-country hunting in winter.

Unit 14
Customs and Quarantines

Part I Pre-listening

Puzzles

Complete the following word puzzles according to the clues given below.

Up: a kind of popular music
Down: sound sent back
Left: hard green stone
Right: nought

Pronunciation

Listen and choose the right explanation of the sentences you hear.

1. A. He wants to send a message.
   B. She wants to send a message.
   C. He wants a message from her.
2. A. The red one is cheaper.
   B. The red one is more expensive.
   C. They both cost the same.
3. A. They are watching TV together.
   B. They are doing different things at the same time.
   C. Both of them are doing their homework.
4. A. He is calling at 10 o'clock.
   B. He is still calling now.
   C. He is not calling now.
5. A. Ellen sings better.
   B. Mike sings better than Ellen.
   C. Both of them sing well.
6. A. Frank likes fishing more than hiking.
   B. Emma likes fishing better.
   C. Emma likes both fishing and hiking. .
7. A. A sales agent came out of the office.
   B. The woman was a travel agent.

C. The woman came out of the agent's office.

8. A. They're talking about an actor.

   B. They are talking about me.

   C. I really know what they are talking about.

Part II   Listening In

Responses

You will hear five sentences. Listen carefully and select the best response to the question or statement.

1. A. No, you don't have to.

   B. Yes, I'm Mr. Claire.

   C. I don't think so.

2. A. Sure, I'll do it now.

   B. I got out of the farm.

   C. I left the case at home.

3. A. At the back of the building.

   B. Around ten o'clock, I think.

   C. I think he is in the meeting now.

4. A. I'll see you this afternoon.

   B. It's been rescheduled for tomorrow.

   C. No, it's out of service.

5. A. I have turned in my report.

   B. I'll travel first class.

   C. If you don't mind.

Questions: General Information about CIQ

You will hear some sentences. Listen carefully and select the best response to the question.

1. How many channels are there at an airport?

   A. customs   B. immigration   C. quarantine   D. above all

2. What is the function of Customs?

   A. To control the outflow and inflow of the currency and products.

   B. To control and check people entering and leaving the country.

   C. To check people, plants and animals, aircraft and cargo for infectious disease.

D. Above all

3. How many exits are there to go through customs?
   A. 1   B. 2   C. 3   D. 4
4. How many categories can quarantine be divided into?
   A. 1   B. 2   C. 3   D. 4
5. Where will the immigration officer mark his check on flight crew's passport?
   A. On the right of their names
   B. On the left of their names
   C. On the upside of their names
   D. On the downside of their names

Dialogue: My Customs Declaration

Word Study

effects: things that someone owns, or personal things

carton: a large container with smaller containers of goods inside it

be subject to: to force someone or something to experience something unpleasant

Listen to the following dialogue and choose the proper answer to the question.

1. Which item did he not buy?
   A. cigar   B. perfume   C. cognac   D. cloth
2. What's the limitation of the cigarettes and cigars?
   A. 25 cigarettes and 200 cigars
   B. 200 cigarettes and 25 cigars
   C. 1 box of cigars and 2 cartons of cigarettes
   D. 2 boxes of cigars and 1 carton of cigarettes
3. Which items did he choose to pay at last?
   A. watch and cloth
   B. 1 carton of cigarettes and a box of cigars
   C. watch and cigars
   D. cigars and cloth
4. Which of the following statements is true?
   A. He had nothing to declare.
   B. He bought some wine as gifts.
   C. He paid the duty to the customs agent.
   D. He carried a few gifts as well as his personal belongings.

Unit 14 Customs and Quarantines

Dialogue: China Immigration Clearance

Listen to the dialogue and complete the information in the card.

```
外国人入境卡
ARRIVAL CARD                               请交边防检查官员查核
                                            For Immigration clearance

姓 Family name _____        名 Given names _____
国籍 Nationality _____        护照号码 Passport No. _____
在华住址 Intended Address in China _____        男 Male ☐  女 Female ☐
出生日期 Date of birth  年Year 月Month 日Day
签证号码 Visa No. _____
签证签发地 Place of Visa Issuance _____

入境事由(只能填写一项) Purpose of visit (one only)
会议/商务 Conference/Business ☐    访问 Visit ☐    观光/休闲 Sightseeing/in leisure ☐
探亲访友 Visiting friends or relatives ☐    就业 Employment ☐    学习 Study ☐
航班号/船名/车次 Flight No./Ship's name/Train No. _____
返回常住地 Return home ☐    定居 Settle down ☐    其他 others ☐

以上申明真实准确。
I hereby declare that the statement given above is true and accurate.
                                            签名 Signature _____
```

Part III   Listening and Understanding

14-3

Passage: Peoples Republic of China Duty Free Allowances Summary

> **Word Study**
>
> alcoholic : connected with or containing alcohol
>
> spirits: a strong alcoholic drink such as whisky or brandy
>
> the authorities: people or organizations that are in charge of a particular country

Listen to the following passage and choose the proper answer to the question.

1. Which city do these rules apply to?

   A. Hangzhou   B. Taiwan   C. Hong Kong   D. Macau

2. How many cigarettes differences you can take when your stay is less than 6 months and excess of 6 months?

   A. 400   B. 600   C. 1200   D. 200

3. You need to pay for the duty if you're taking _____ out of China.

   A. A 50cl bottle of spirits for stays within 6 months

   B. 5kg of silver for stays within 6 months

   C. 400 cigarettes for stays more than 6 months

   D. 2x75cl bottles of alcoholic for stays more than 6 months

4. Which of the following statements is correct?

   A. Things for personal use are duty free.

   B. Gifts must not be declared.

   C. Valuable items must be checked if you don't complete the luggage declaration form.

   D. Keep all receipts for valuable effects when entering China.

5. Which of the following statements is not correct?

   A. Make sure you complete a passenger luggage declaration form on arrival.

   B. Keep ALL receipts for valuable items and effects you buy while in China.

   C. For stays in excess of 6 months, you can bring two bottles of alcoholic.

   D. You can bring a reasonable amount of perfume for personal use no matter how many months you stay.

Passage: Macau Duty Free Allowances Summary

Word Study

administrative : connected with organizing the work of a business or an institution

deem: consider

abv: alcohol by volume

providing: used to say that something will only be possible if something else happens or is done

Listen to the following passage and fill the form about the allowances of each item.

Items	Allowance
Alcoholic liquor/spirit with an alcoholic strength above 30% (liter)	
Cigarettes	
Manufactured Tobacco (grams)	
Jewelry	
computer	
Cigar	

Listen to the passage again and answer the following questions.

1. Why is traveling from China mainland to Macau subject to customs check?

2. Write down all the duty free items which are mentioned in this passage.

3. On what condition are other items not restricted to import?

4. How much tax free of the items you may bring in Macau?(MOP)

5. Why all the gifts and presents purchased will not be subject to tax?

Part IV   Listening and Enjoying

Passage: European airlines

Listen to the following passage and choose the proper answer to the question.
1. Which of the following statements is correct?
   A. Each European airline has the same service standard.
   B. Every flight from European airlines is punctual.
   C. Passengers feel comfortable with European attendants' service.
   D. European airlines don't like their attendants to show any individuality.
2. What service standards in European airlines are similar?
   A. Punctuality   B. Safety
   C. Eyes on details   D. All of the above.
3. What does "priority" mean in the second paragraph?
   A. importance   B. attempt
   C. possibility   D. direction
4. What does the fact show that logos on the cups are put in the same direction?
   A. European airlines are strict to their attendants.
   B. European airlines pay much attention to the detail in their service.
   C. European people like drinking tea.
   D. European attendants show their individuality in this way.
5. European airlines value their attendants on the following abilities except _____.
   A. Positive attitude   B. Cooperation

C. Team work   D. Individuality above general standards

Culture Perspective: Hulun Buir Grassland

Listen to the following passage and fill in the missing words.

Hulun Buir Grassland situates in the west of Greater Xing'an Mountains, _____ an area of about 100,000 square kilometers. Natural grassland accounts for 80% of this area. It has been called "the _____ of Chinese northern nomadic people".

Hulun Buir Grassland is famous for its beautiful scenery and rich _____ resources. There are more beautiful things than the eye can _____: twisting river, Mongolian yurts, shrubs, blue sky, herds of cattle and sheep on the _____ grassland. It feels like a _____ and refreshing picture. Winters here are quite long and bitterly cold with heavy ice and snow, while summers are temperate and comfortably cool. It's _____ of the title of summer resort.

Visitors can watch _____ with local features, like wrestling, dancing or Barhu wedding(a traditional Mongolian wedding ceremony). You can also try the daily activities such as milking cows, shearing sheep or _____ milk tea, etc.

It is also a place where visitors can experience the _____ customs and cultures of ethnic groups like Ewenk, Orogen, Daur and Russian minorities.

Keys and Audio scripts

Unit 8 Meal and Drink Service

Part I   Pre-listening

Matching

Listen to the following sentences and match them with the pictures below.

Tape scripts

A. Ticket, please!

B. Welcome aboard! We hope you enjoy your flight with us today!

C. The aeroplane has landed.

D. Mr. Bull is taking Peppa and her family to the airport.

E. This is the X-Ray machine. It's a machine that looks inside things.

F. We hope you will enjoy your flight. Please fasten your seat belts.

(1) [D]

(2) [A]

(3) [E]

(4) [B]

(5) [F]

(6) [C]

Pronunciation

I. Directions: The following boxes are going to introduce four types of the loss of plosives. You'll hear four groups of words and then try to underline where the loss of plosives occurs.

> When a plosive is close to another one, the loss of plosive happens in the former. Six plosives include:/p/ /b/ /t/ /d/ /k/ /g/
> Example: O<u>c</u>tober
> /ɒ<u>k</u>'təʊbə/

> When a plosive is close to fricative consonant, the incomplete loss of plosive happens. Ten fricative consonants include: /f/ /v/ /s/ /z/ /ʃ/ /ʒ/ /θ/ /ð/ /r/ /h/
> Example: as<u>k</u> for
> /ɑ:s<u>k</u> ˈfɔ:/

pra<u>c</u>tice　Se<u>p</u>tember　goo<u>d</u>bye

u<u>p</u>date　　co<u>ck</u>tail　　loo<u>k</u>ed

e<u>x</u>ist　　a<u>d</u>vice　　a<u>c</u>cept

su<u>cc</u>ess　frien<u>d</u>ship　boo<u>k</u>shelf

> When a plosive is close to affricates, the incomplete loss of plosive happens. Two affricates include: /tʃ/ /dʒ/
> Example: har<u>d</u> job
> /hɑr<u>d</u> dʒɔb/

> When a plosive is close to nasals, the incomplete loss of plosive happens. Three nasals include: /m/ /n/ /ŋ/
> Example: a<u>t</u> night
> /æ<u>t</u> naɪt/

pi<u>c</u>ture　le<u>c</u>ture　　o<u>b</u>ject

su<u>b</u>ject　a goo<u>d</u> job　bes<u>t</u> choice

a<u>d</u>mit　ni<u>ck</u>name　su<u>dd</u>en

cer<u>t</u>ain　mi<u>d</u>night　depar<u>t</u>ment

II. Directions: Listen to the following sentences and underline where the loss of plosives occurs.

1. Teacher asks us to wri<u>te</u> down our names on the blackboard.
2. When you have free time, please sto<u>p</u> by for a chat.
3. Chinese culture is qui<u>te</u> different from western culture.
4. When I see these ol<u>d</u> photos, I always think of my childhood.
5. Do you like dee<u>p</u> red or ligh<u>t</u> red?
6. I think this is a goo<u>d</u> chance to improve your ability.
7. Grea<u>t</u> changes have taken place in China.
8. It is really a pleasan<u>t</u> journey with you.
9. The prince and princess finally go<u>t</u> married and lived happily.

10. Lucy and Lily are my ol**d** friends.

Part II   Listening In

Responses

You will hear five sentences. Listen carefully and select the best response to the questions or statements.

1. Do I have to book in advance for the hotel?

   A. Yes, it's advisable.

   B. My pleasure.

   C. You don't need to think so.

2. What happens if I return those books late?

   A. Sorry, I won't.

   B. Keep doing like this.

   C. You will be fined.

3. Could you tell me what I have to do to join the club?

   A. Please fill out some forms and bring your ID card.

   B. It takes you about forty minutes to get our club.

   C. Our services are the best.

4. Do you feel like having seafood tonight?

   A. After that lunch, I am not sure I can eat anything!

   B. Take it easy.

   C. Hurry up, will you?

5. Somebody's been leaving this door unlocked.

   A. Don't mention it!

   B. Sounds good!

   C. Don't look at me.

Dialogue: Serving the Food

I. Listen to the dialogue and try to tell whether the following statements are true or not.

Tape scripts

Passenger: Excuse me. What time is dinner served?

Flight attendant: We will start the meal service 30 minutes after take-off.

Passenger: Oh, I can't wait that long. I am starving now.

Flight attendant: Let me get you some snacks as soon as we take off.

Passenger: That will be great. Thank you.

Flight attendant: We are serving food, Sir. Would you put down your tray table, please?

Passenger: Sure. What do you serve for dinner?

Flight attendant: We have pork rice or beef noodle.

Passenger: I am a vegetarian and my wife is a Muslim. Do you have any special meals?

Flight attendant: How about vegetables stewed with rice?

Passenger: That sounds great.

Flight attendant: Sir, you can order a special meal when you book your ticket if you have some special need.

Passenger: I will. I forgot to order our meal in advance.

Flight attendant: OK. What kinds of salads do you want, fruit or vegetable?

Passenger: Is this vegetable salad pure vegetarian?

Flight attendant: I'm afraid not. It has dried shrimp.

Passenger: I didn't expect it to be this greasy. Then fruit salad, please.

(Several minutes later)

Passenger: Attendant, please!

Flight attendant: Is there a problem with your dish?

Passenger: The fruit in this salad is not fresh and the salad is too dry. Besides, the chicken is all burned.

Flight attendant: I am terribly sorry. We will make you another one right away.

1. The passenger asks the flight attendant about the time for taking off. **(F)**

2. The passenger has put down his tray table already before the flight attendant tells to do so. **(F)**

3. The passenger will remember to order a special meal next time. **(T)**

4. The passenger finally chooses fruits salad because he likes the greasy food. **(F)**

5. The flight attendant solves the problem the passenger complains about. **(T)**

II. Listen to the dialogue again and choose the proper answer to the questions.

1. How long does the flight attendant begin to serve dinner after take-off?

    A. 13 minutes.

    B. 30 minutes.

    C. 40 minutes.

    D. 60 minutes.

2. What kinds of food does the flight attendant promise to bring to the passenger as soon as the plane takes off?

    A. Some drinks.

    B. Some salads.

    C. Some desserts.

    D. Some snacks.

3. How many main dishes does the flight offer?

    A. One.

B. Two.

C. Three.

D. Four.

4. Why does the passenger finally decide to have fruits salad instead of vegetable salad?

　A. He is a vegetarian.

　B. He is on the diet.

　C. He doesn't like shrimp.

　D. He thinks fruits are fresher than vegetables.

5. The passenger complains about the services **EXCEPT** that _____.

　A. the attendant keeps passenger waiting too long

　B. the fruits in this salad are not fresh

　C. the salad is too dry

　D. the chicken is all burned

Dialogue: Serving the Drink

I. Listen to the following dialogue and choose the proper answer to the question.

Tape scripts

Flight attendant: What can I do for you, sir? Would you like something to drink?

Passenger A: I haven't got any drink yet. I'm a little thirsty now.

Flight attendant: Sorry, sir. You were sleeping while we served. I didn't want to interrupt you.

Passenger A: Well, what is available on board?

Flight attendant: We have coffee, tea, juice, or milk.

Passenger A: Ok, Juice. I want to have something sour.

Flight attendant: We have apple, orange, and peach. Which one do you prefer?

Passenger A: Orange.

Flight attendant: Here you are. How about you?

Passenger B: Since our destination is Beijing, I'd like to try something typically Chinese. I want to have some tea.

Flight attendant: Well, we have Dragon Well tea from Hangzhou and Biluochun from Jiangsu. Do you want to have a try?

Passenger B: I have heard a lot about Dragon Well tea before, but I have no idea about the taste, so I'd like to try it this time. By the way, is there any black tea in China?

Flight attendant: Yes. The most famous black tea is Oolong. It can help people lose weight, but green tea is also a good choice.

Passenger B: Thank you for your brief introduction.

1. According to the dialogue, what kind of drink is **NOT** served on the plane?

　A. Coffee.

B. Beer.
   C. Juice.
   D. Tea.
2. What was the man doing while the drink served?
   A. Eating.
   B. Reading.
   C. Sleeping.
   D. Chatting.
3. Why does the man choose tea?
   A. Because he has drunk tea before.
   B. Because he likes to try something different.
   C. Because he likes to try something typically Chinese.
   D. Because he likes to try something sour.
4. What kinds of tea does the second man finally order?
   A. **Dragon Well tea.**
   B. Biluochun.
   C. Black tea.
   D. Green tea.
5. If people want to lose weight, they should try _____.
   A. Dragon Well tea
   B. Biluochun
   C. Black tea
   D. **Green tea**

II. Listen to the dialogue again and then fill in the blanks.
1. I'm a little **thirsty** now.
2. I didn't want to **interrupt** you.
3. Well, what is **available** on board?
4. I want to have something **sour**.
5. Since our **destination** is Beijing, I'd like to try something typically Chinese.

Part III   Listening and Understanding

Passage: Mobile Phones are Allowed on Planes — For or Against?

I. Listen to the passage and try to tell whether the following statements are true or not.

Tape scripts

Recently, according to a statement issued by the CAAC, a number of domestic airlines have announced that passengers will be permitted to use in-flight portable electronic devices as long as they have airplane mode switched on. Such policies not only make flying more convenient for passengers, but represent huge progress in civil aviation industry. The in-flight Wi-Fi market in China is expected to enter a rapid growth period in the next few years. Most domestic routes will be equipped with Wi-Fi services. However, we cannot ignore some behaviors that violate the rights of others, such as noises made by some passengers watching videos without earphones. There is a risk that this uncivilized behavior is more likely to lead to disorder or chaos, such as quarrels even fights. How to solve this problem? First of all, passengers should be aware of what can be done during the flight. That is to say, passengers can kill time by using mobile phones, tablets and laptops, but the sound they make should not affect others. In addition, it is necessary for the authorities to lay down some rules. People's behavior on airplanes should be regulated and then their legal rights can be protected. Only by joint efforts from passengers and authority can the passengers enjoy their flights and public order be maintained.

1. The new rule allows passengers to use their phones on the plane but they have airplane mode switched on . **(T)**

2. Most domestic routes have been equipped with Wi-Fi services. **(F)**

3. It doesn't matter that passengers watch videos without using earphones. **(F)**

4. People have already known what they should do in flight so authorities don't need make rules. **(F)**

5. Passenger and authorities should make joint efforts to maintain order during the flight. **(T)**

II. Listen to the passage again and try to finish the summary.

Topic: Mobile Phones are Allowed on Planes

For

• making flying more **1. convenient**

• represent huge **2. progress**

Against

• some behaviors that **3. violate** the rights of others

• some behaviors that are more likely to lead to **4. disorder** or **5. chaos**

Suggestions

• passengers should **6. be aware of** what can be done during the flight

• authorities should **7. lay down** some rules

Effects

• People's behavior on airplanes should be **8. regulated** and legal rights can be **9. protected**

• public order can be **10. maintained**

Keys and Audio scripts

Passage: C919, Chinese-made Airbus, Our National Pride

I. Listen to the passage and match the information in the box with the following sentences.

Tape scripts

On May 5, 2017, jet C919, the first large passenger aircraft designed and built by China, made its maiden flight, with 158 seats and a standard range of 4,075 kilometers, leaving from Shanghai Pudong International Airport. This flight was not only a significant step for Chinese aviation industry, but also could be a strong option for global carriers in decades to come. It was expected to compete with the updated Airbus 320 and Boeing 737 that currently dominate the market. Boeing and Airbus are very mature aircraft manufacturers; however, C919 focuses on innovation and technological breakthroughs, and then it will be a strong competitor in this field. In addition, being economical and comfortable also makes it more competitive.

China has been investing heavily in commercial passenger jet manufacturing. In 2007, plans to develop a domestic large passenger jet were approved by the State Council. In November 2015, the first C919 jet rolled off the assembly line. In March, the aircraft passed a major technical assessment, the last step before its maiden flight. The process usually takes one to two months. A total of 23 foreign and domestic customers have placed orders for 570 aircraft, according to the Commercial Aircraft Corporation of China.

> a. Boeing and Airbus
> b. China
> c. Airbus 320 and Boeing 737
> d. 23 foreign and domestic customers
> e. C919

1. **(e)** the first large passenger aircraft designed and built by China.
2. **(a)** very mature aircraft manufacturers.
3. **(d)** have placed orders for 570 aircraft.
4. **(c)** currently dominate the market.
5. **(b)** has been investing heavily in commercial passenger jet manufacturing.

II. Listen to the dialogue again and try to tell whether the following statements are true or not.

1. Jet C919 has more than 150 seats. **(T)**
2. Jet C919 finally landed on the Shanghai Pudong International Airport. **(F)**
3. Jet C919 had become a strong competitor with the updated Airbus 320 and 737. **(F)**
4. In November 2007, the first C919 jet rolled off the assembly line. **(F)**
5. The last step before a plane maiden flight is technical assessment. **(T)**

III. Listen to the dialogue again and choose the proper answer to the question.

1. The flight has great importance in many aspects **EXCEPT** that _____.

   A. it means a significant step for Chinese aviation industry.

   B. it is the first large passenger aircraft designed and built by China.

   C. it offers a strong option for global carriers in decades to come.

   D. it has become a mature aircraft manufacturer.

2. Which one is not the feature of C919?

   A. It focuses on innovation.

   B. It focuses on technological breakthroughs.

   C. It is economical and comfortable.

   D. It currently dominates the market.

3. According to the passage, which kind of airplane is invested heavily in China?

   A. Military jet manufacturing.

   B. Goods delivery jet manufacturing.

   C. Commercial passenger jet manufacturing.

   D. Private jet manufacturing.

4. How long does the technical assessment usually take?

   A. One to two days.

   B. One to two weeks.

   C. One to two months.

   D. One to two years.

5. If customers want to purchase the C919, who can they find to ask for?

   A. State Council.

   B. China's national carrier Air China.

   C. Boeing and Airbus.

   D. Commercial Aircraft Corporation of China (COMAC).

Part IV Listening and Enjoying

Cultural Perspective: Dining Etiquette In Western Country

Listen to the passage and try to tell whether the following statements are true or not.

Tape scripts

In the western countries, dining etiquette is considered as an important part of social manners. It is necessary for visitors from other countries to learn proper manners at dinner time to win respect.

Table setting rules

For a formal dinner, proper table setting is very important. The general rules are as follows.

A plate is placed in the middle and forks should be arranged to the left of the plate while knives should be placed to the right. Spoons should be arranged next to the knives. Napkin is usually folded into a long rectangle and placed to the left of the forks. When seated, one should unfold the napkin and place it across the lap.

Courses of dishes

A full course dinner usually consists of many dishes. The first is a starter or appetizer. It is a type of food or drink that can stimulate dinners' appetite. After that, the main course is served. Meat is the main ingredient in the main course, with some sauces, vegetables, perhaps some potatoes and bread. In addition, wines are usually served with the main dish at the same time. There is one simple rule to order the wine: white wine for white meat such as chicken and fish while red wine for red meat such as beef. Dessert comes at the end of the dinner. There are some sweet food on the dinner table, such as fruit, ice-cream, pie, pudding, etc..

Dinner etiquette

Generally, British people would like to host people in their homes. It is polite to arrive 10 to 15 minutes later than the appointed time to dinner at home in England, but to arrive on time in Scotland and Wales. In the Unites States, if one has not finished eating, cross the knife and fork on the plate with the fork over the knife. If the host folds his or her napkin, that means the meal is over.

1. A plate is placed in the middle and forks should be arranged to the right of the plate while knives should be placed to the left. **(F)**

2. A full course dinner usually consists of starter, main course and dessert. **(T)**

3. Bread is the main ingredient in the main course. **(F)**

4. White wine should go with white meat while the red wine should go with red meat . **(T)**

5. It is impolite to arrive 10 to 15 minutes later than the appointed time to dinner at home in England. **(F)**

A Poem: I remember, I remember

by Thomas Hood

I remember, I remember,
The house where I was born,
The little window where the sun,
Came peeping in at morn;
He never came a wink too soon,
Nor brought too long a day,
But now I often wish the night,
Had borne my breath away!

I remember, I remember,

The roses red and white,

The violets, and the lily-cups,

Those flowers made of light!

The lilacs where the robin built,

And where my brother set,

The laburnum on his birth-day,

The tree is living yet!

I remember, I remember,

Where I was used to swing,

And thought the air must rush as fresh,

To swallows on the wing;

My spirit flew in feathers then,

That is so heavy now,

And summer pools could hardly cool,

The fever on my brow!

I remember, I remember,

The fir-trees dark and high;

I used to think their slender tops,

Were close against the sky:

It was a childish ignorance,

But now it's little joy,

To know I'm further off from the heaven,

Than when I was a boy.

Unit 9　In-flight Entertainment

Part I　Pre-listening

Tongue Twister

Coffee Pot

All I want is a proper cup of coffee made in a proper copper coffee pot, you can believe it or not, but I just want a cup of coffee in a proper coffee pot.

Tin coffee pots or iron coffee pots are of no use to me.

If I can't have a proper cup of coffee in a proper copper coffee pot, I'll have a cup of tea!

Pronunciation

I. Directions: You'll hear one word read from each group. Listen carefully and tick out the word you hear.

1. **A. head**	B. had	C. said	D. sad
2. **A. hut**	B. heart	C. cart	D. cat
3. A. full	B. pull	C. pool	**D. pour**
4. A. spots	B. shot	C. short	**D. sports**
5. A. isle	**B. ale**	C. oil	D. aisle
6. A. fail	B. foil	**C. file**	D. feel
7. **A. loud**	B. load	C. out	D. loot
8. A. cheers	B. sheer	**C. chairs**	D. share
9. A. cold	**B. gold**	C. coat	D. goat
10. **A. pack**	B. peg	C. bag	D. back

II. Assimilation

Directions: Listen carefully and repeat.

◎ light (p) blue

◎ that (p) mall

◎ get them [gettem]

◎ read these [ri:ddi:z]

Think and try to find out some more words like this.

◎ quite (k) good

◎ that case [ðækkeis]

Part II   Listening In

Responses:

You will hear five sentences. Listen carefully and select the best response to the question or statement.

1. Excuse me, Miss. Can you show me how to use the headset?

   A. I think so.

   B. Sure. Let me show you.

   C. OK. I will get you another one.

2. Can you help me adjust it? I want to listen to music.

   A. Yes, please.

   B. Of course. Here you are.

   C. You can press this button and select the channel you like.

3. Do you have something to read?

   A. Sorry, I don't know.

   B. Yes. We have magazines.

   C. Here you are.

4. I prefer light classics. Which channel is it on?

   A. The fourth one.

   B. Yes. There are several kinds of music.

   C. Yes. It's very nice.

5. Would you care for a newspaper, sir?

   A. What newspaper do you have?

   B. Thank you. I will.

   C. I see. Let me try.

Dialogue: Supplementary Reading Material

Listen to the following dialogue and choose the proper answer to the question.

Tape scripts

Passenger: Excuse me, Miss. I have watched all these movies. Do you have any supplementary reading material?

Flight attendant: Yes, we do. Would you care for a newspaper, sir?

Passenger: What newspaper do you have?

Flight attendant: We have China Daily and The New York Times.

Passenger: Do you have the Washington Post?

Flight attendant: No, I'm sorry. But I do have the China Daily.

Passenger: Then I suppose that will have to do.

Flight attendant: Here you are, sir. We also have magazine Victory, the CAAC In-Flight Magazine and so on. Would you like a couple of them?

Passenger: No, thank you. By the way, do you have anything for my four-year-old son?

Flight attendant: Yes. We have child packs that contain crayons, story-books and other animated movies.

Passenger: Great! How considerate of you. Thank you very much.

Flight attendant: You are welcome. I will come back shortly.

1. At first, the passenger would like to have a copy of _____ to read.

   A. Washington Post.

   B. China Daily.

   C. The New York Times.

   D. CAAC In-Flight Magazine.

2. How old is the passenger's child?

A. Five.

B. Fifteen.

C. Four.

D. Fourteen.

3. A child pack doesn't contain _____ .

A. animated movies

B. crayons

C. fruits

D. story-books

Dialogue: How to Use the Headsets?

Listen to the dialogue and fill in the missing words.

Tape scripts

Passenger: Excuse me, Miss. **1. Can you give me a hand**?

Flight attendant: Yes, of course. What can I do for you?

Passenger: I don't know how to use the headsets. Will you tell me how to use them?

Flight attendant: OK. Let me **2. show** you. First, put the **3. plugs** into your ears. Then, put the jack into this **4. hole** at your **5. armrest**. And last, press the button and select the channel you like.

Passenger: Can you help me **6. adjust** it? I want to listen to music.

Flight attendant: Certainly, there is rock music, **7. classical** music, opera and so on. **8. Which programs do you prefer?**

Passenger: I prefer rock music. I'm **9. crazy** about it. I often listen to my iPod while running.

Flight attendant: OK. Please press the button to select the 1st channel. I hope you will enjoy yourself.

Passenger: **10. That's very kind of you.** Thank you very much.

Flight attendant: You're welcome.

Part III Listening and Understanding

Dialogue: Lift the Screen up

I. Listen to the dialogue and try to tell whether the following statements are true or not.

Tape scripts

Flight attendant: (announcement) Ladies and gentlemen, now we will be showing programs such as film, music and others. We hope you will enjoy them. Please use the headsets in the seat pocket in front of you. Choose which channel corresponds with the programs that you wish to watch. You may ask your cabin attendants for assistance. Thank you!

Passenger: Excuse me, Miss.

Flight attendant: Yes. Can I help you?

Passenger: I enjoy listening to music. Music is the most beautiful language in the world. Can I have a pair of headsets please?

Flight attendant: Yes, of course. Here you are.

Passenger: Miss, one of the headsets doesn't work. Could you please change it for me?

Flight attendant: No problem. Can I check them for you?

Yes, they aren't working. I will get you another set. Give me a minute…Here you are.

Passenger: Thank you very much. By the way, I want to watch a movie. But, how to lift the screen up?

Flight attendant: Let me show you. First open the armrest, press this button and you can lift it up. After that you slide this cover backwards so you can see the TV unit, then you just press it to release it. Now you can turn it to suit you and press this switch on the arm.

Passenger: How considerate of you. What do you recommend?

Flight attendant: There is an interesting movie on channel one. It is supposed to be really good. I hope you will enjoy your movie.

Passenger: I see. Thank you very much.

Flight attendant: You are welcome.

1. The flight attendant told the passenger that the music is the most beautiful language in the world. **(F)**

2. The passenger asked for another pair of headsets to bring them home. **(F)**

3. The passenger doesn't want to watch a movie. **(F)**

4. The passenger doesn't know how to lift the screen up. **(T)**

5. There is an interesting movie on channel four. **(F)**

II. Listen to the dialogue again and fill in the missing words.

A. The announcement

Ladies and gentlemen, now we will be **1. showing** programs such as film, music and others. We hope you will enjoy them. Please use the **2. headsets** in the seat pocket in front of you. **3. Choose** which channel **4. corresponds** with the programs that you wish to watch. You may ask your cabin attendants for **5. assistance**. Thank you!

B. How to lift the screen up?

Let me show you. First open the **6. armrest**, press this **7. button** and you can lift it up. After that you **8. slide** this cover backwards so you can see the TV unit, then you just press it to **9. release** it. Now you can turn it to suit you and press this **10. switch** on the arm.

Keys and Audio scripts

Passage: The Entertainment System

I. Listen to the passage and try to tell whether the following statements are true or not.

Tape scripts

All airplanes are equipped with an entertainment system. It provides the passengers with varied interesting video and audio programs during the flight.

The passenger entertainment system transmits pre-recorded audio and video programs to the passengers. They can listen to the audio programs through the headsets connected to the passenger control units. The passenger entertainment system comprises audio reproducers and the passenger control units. Each of the audio reproducers gives a number of different music programs and the passenger control unit is installed on the armrest of each seat.

On some flights, there are more than 10 channels of video and audio programs. The passengers choose the program they want to listen to or watch by pressing channel push-buttons. They can adjust the volume by pushing the upper or the lower volume push-buttons. The programs are designed and delivered by the airlines. Some channels are available for first and business class passengers and others are available for the economy class passengers. Among these channels are feature films such as drama, classic, comedy, romance, thriller, adventure and many video programs such as travelogues, cartoons and sports. Apart from audio portion of the films, there are many other programs for audio entertainment. A variety of music tracks are available in some medium and long-range flights, such as classical music, current popular hits, rock and roll, jazz, light music and opera.

On many airplanes, especially in first and business class cabins, the video programs can be watched on a small screen that is attached to each seat. It is either on the seat back in front of each passenger or in the armrest. On other types of airplanes, there are four or five large screens in the cabin.

Before the program, the cabin attendants distribute the headsets to each of the passengers so that they can listen to the sound tracks of the video or the audio program. The passengers can open the plastic bag, take the headsets out, put it on and plug it into the passenger control unit on the armrest. They can then set up the TV screen and choose the program they like best.

At the beginning of the flight, the cabin attendants may be called upon to assist passengers with the operation of the headsets, locating the proper channels for the audio portion of the film, or replacing faulty headset equipment. During the programs, the cabin attendants walk along the cabin aisle as usual, at least once every fifteen minutes.

1. The entertainment system provides the passengers with varied interesting video and audio programs during the flight. **(T)**

2. The passengers choose the program they want to listen to or watch by pressing the call button. **(F)**

3. A variety of music tracks are available in some flights, such as classical music, current

83

popular hits, rock and roll, jazz, light music and opera. **(T)**

4. Before the program, the captain should distribute the headsets to each of the passengers. **(F)**

5. During the programs, the cabin attendants walk along the cabin aisle as usual, at least once every ten minutes. **(F)**

II. Listen carefully to the following passage again and choose the proper answers to the question.

1. The passenger can listen to the audio programs through the headsets connected to _____.

    A. the passenger audio reproducers

    B. the passenger channel push-buttons

    C. the passenger control units

    D. The passenger screen

2. The passenger control unit is installed on the _____ of each seat.

    A. armrest

    B. back

    C. top

    D. channel

3. The passenger can adjust the volume by _____.

    A. pushing the upper or the lower volume push-buttons.

    B. pushing the upper or the lower channel push-buttons.

    C. pushing the upper or the lower audio push-buttons.

    D. pushing the upper or the lower video push-buttons.

4. The screen is either _____ or in the armrest.

    A. on the tray table in front of each passenger

    B. on the window shade in front of each passenger

    C. near the reading light in front of each passenger

    D. on the seat back in front of each passenger

5. At the beginning of the flight, the cabin attendants may be called upon to assist passengers, except _____.

    A. showing the operation of the headsets

    B. replacing faulty headset equipment

    C. singing a great song

    D. locating the proper channels

III. Listen to the passage again and fill in the missing words.

1. Each of the audio **reproducers** gives a number of different music programs and the passenger control unit is **installed** on the armrest of each seat.

2. Among these channels are **feature** films such as drama, **classic**, comedy, romance, thriller, **adventure** and many video programs such as **travelogues**, cartoons and sports.

3. On many airplanes, **especially** in first and business class cabins, the video programs can be watched on a small screen that is **attached** to each seat.

4. The passengers can open the **plastic bag**, take the headsets out, put it on and **plug** it into the passenger control unit on the armrest.

Passage: Notting Hill
Listen to the passage and fill in the missing words.
Tape scripts

Can a beautiful and **1. internationally** famous American actress find happiness with an **2. old-fashioned** and unattractive man, a British bookstore clerk? Yes, she can—**3. at least** for a while in Notting Hill. William Thacker is a **4. bookseller** at a shop in the Notting Hill district in West London, who **5. shares** a house with an eccentric Welsh friend, Spike. One day, William is minding the store when he sees Anna Scott, a lovely and **6. well-known** actress from the United States who is in London working on a film.

She buys a book from William, and she is polite and **7. charming**. Their relationship would logically end there, if William didn't run out a few minutes later and buy some juice. When quickly going back to the shop, he runs across Anna on the street, **8. spilling** juice all over her blouse. Since he lives nearby, William politely offers to let her stop by his house to **9. clean up**; since William seems harmless enough, Anna agrees. When Anna has to stop back to pick up a bag she left at William's house, they kiss—just in time for Spike to show up. A **10. romance** slowly blooms as his friends and family wonder what he's doing dating a movie star. What will happen to them?

Part IV Listening and Enjoying

Cultural Perspective: Peking Opera
Listen carefully to the following passage and try to find out the proper answers.
Tape scripts

Beijing opera or Peking opera is a kind of Chinese opera which arose in the mid-19th century and was extremely popular in the Qing Dynasty court. It is widely regarded as one of the cultural treasures of China. Beijing and Tianjin are respected as the base cities of Peking opera in the north while shanghai is the base in the south.

Although it is called Beijing opera, its origins are not in Beijing but in the Chinese provinces of Anhui and Hubei. Beijing opera got its two main melodies, Xipi and Erhuang, from Anhui and Hubei operas.

There are four main roles in Peking Opera: Sheng, Dan, Jing, Chou. The three roles other than the second role represent male characters. There is an explanation about why the roles take the names above. It is said that they were chosen to have opposite meanings to their Chinese characters. Sheng in Chinese may mean "strange" or "rare", but the chief male role is a well known character. Dan, which means "morning" or "masculine", is contrary to the feminine nature of the characters. Jing means "clean", but in fact the paintings on their faces make the characters look unclean but colorful. And Chou in Chinese sometimes represents the animal "ox", which, in some senses, is slow and silent—in contrast, the Chou characters are usually quick and talkative.

When it comes to types of facial makeup in Beijing opera, it is a national cosmetic with special features. As each historical figure or a certain type of person has a certain type, just like we should sing and perform according to the score, so they are called "types of facial makeup in operas." It is reported to originate from masks.

1. Peking opera is a kind of Chinese opera which arose in the _____ century.

   A. mid-18th

   B. mid-19th

   C. mid-20th

   D. mid-21st

2. Beijing and _____ are respected as the base cities of Peking opera in the north.

   A. Tianjin

   B. Shanghai

   C. Hunan

   D. Anhui

3. There are _____ main roles in Peking Opera.

   A. Two

   B. Three

   C. Four

   D. Five

4. _____, which means "morning" or "masculine", is contrary to the feminine nature of the characters.

   A. Sheng

   B. Dan

   C. Jing

   D. Chou

5. Which of the following statements is not true?

   A. Beijing opera got its two main melodies, Xipi and Erhuang, from Anhui and Hubei operas.

   B. It is said that the name of the main roles were chosen to have same meanings to their Chinese characters.

   C. Chou in Chinese sometimes represents the animal "ox", which, in some senses, is slow and silent.

D. When it comes to types of facial makeup in Beijing opera, it is a national cosmetic with special feature.

Friends: The One with the Proposal

[Scene: The Hallway, Chandler is running up the stairs and towards his apartment, but Joey is taking out the garbage at the same time and stops him in the hall.]

Joey: Dude!

Chandler: I can't talk to you now, I gotta find Monica!

Joey: She's gone.

Chandler: What?

Joey: She's gone. She had a bag and she left.

Chandler: What are you talking about?

Joey: She was all crying. She-she said you guys want different things, and that and that she needed time to think.

Chandler: Well why didn't you stop her?! Why didn't you just tell her it was a plan?!

Joey: I-I did! I told her everything, Chandler! But she wouldn't believe me.

Chandler: Well where... Where did she go?

Joey: To her parent's I think and she said you shouldn't call her. But if I were you I would.

Chandler: I can't believe I ruined this.

Joey: I am so sorry man.

(He walks dejectedly into his apartment to find it lit with about a thousand candles and Monica standing in the living room.)

Monica: You wanted it to be a surprise.

(He turns to look at Joey who smiles slyly and closes the door leaving them alone.)

Chandler: Oh my God.

(Monica gets down on one knee.)

Monica: Chandler... In all my life... I never thought I would be so lucky. (Starting to cry.) As to...fall in love with my best...my best... There's a reason why girls don't do this!

Chandler: Okay! (He joins her on one knee) Okay! Okay! Oh God, I thought... (Starting to cry, pauses) Wait a minute, I-I can do this. (Pause) I thought that it mattered what I said or where I said it. Then I realized the only thing that matters is that you, (Pause) you make me happier than I ever thought I could be. (Starting to cry again.) And if you'll let me, I will spend the rest of my life trying to make you feel the same way. (Pause as he gets out the ring.) Monica, will you marry me?

Monica: Yes.

(The crowd goes wild as he puts the ring on her finger. They hug and kiss this time as an engaged couple.)

Monica: I knew you were likely to take a wife!

(They hug again.)

Joey: (yelling through the door) Can we come it yet?! We're dying out here!

Monica: Come in! Come in! (Joey, Rachel, and Phoebe burst through the door.) We're engaged!!!

(Everyone screams and has a group hug.)

Rachel: Oh, this is the least jealous I've ever been!

Phoebe: Oh no wait no, this is wrong! Ross isn't here!

Monica: Oh…

Rachel: Oh hell, he's done this three times! He knows what its about!

Joey: Yeah!

(They all hug again.)

Unit 10   Duty-free Sales

Part I   Pre-listening

Idioms

Fill in the blanks and then try to find out their meanings.

1. French **leave**

   Going away without saying good-bye.

2. Irish **promotion**

   Demote.

3. Dutch **comfort**

   Strong drink.

4. Dutch **party**

   A party at which everyone has to pay for himself.

5. **Indian** gift

   The present that you expect to receive from whom have got your present before.

Pronunciation

I. Listen to the following dialogue and underline the contracted words.

Susan: Have you been to Switzerland?

Jim: No, I **haven't**. But I plan to visit there next year.

Susan: Well, **it's** a really picturesque country: wonderful landscape, cultural diversity, global warming, and stunning outdoors.

Jim: Yes, **that's** why **it's** called the world garden. My wife and I like traveling very much. And **she's** working on the schedule in detail.

Susan: **There're** so many things to do and to explore there. **You'll** love it definitely.

Jim: **That'll** be great! I **can't** wait to go.

II. Think and try to find out some other contracted forms.

e.g.

I'd; let's; won't; wouldn't; don't; doesn't

Abbreviation

I. Write down the full name of these abbreviation words according to what you hear.

1. IATA（国际航空运输协会）

   <u>International Air Transport Association</u>

2. AC（中国国际航空公司）

   <u>Air China</u>

3. ATC（空中管制）

   <u>Air Traffic Control</u>

4. UNESCO（联合国教科文组织）

   <u>United Nations Educational Scientific and Cultural Organization</u>

5. ICAO（国际民航协会）

   <u>International Civil Aviation Organization</u>

6. AUX（辅助设备）

   <u>auxiliary</u>

II. Listen and write down the abbreviations.

1. <u> CATA </u>　　China Air Transport Association
2. <u> CAAC </u>　　Civil Aviation Administration of China
3. <u>   ASU   </u>　　Attendant Service Unit
4. <u> ASAP </u>　　As soon as possible
5. <u>   ATE   </u>　　Automatic Test Equipment
6. <u>   BAT   </u>　　Battery

Part II   Listening In

Responses

You will hear five sentences. Listen carefully and select the best response to the question or statement.

1. What color would you like to choose?

   A. Yes, I think so.

   B. I'd choose the smaller one.

   C. I like purple better.

2. Can I have a look at the samples?

A. Sure, you can.

B. Yes, you can have some apples.

C. It's behind the table.

3. Do I have to park the car here or outside there?

   A. No, there's no parking space.

   B. Either will be fine.

   C. It's not allowed.

4. Can I change the time for the interview?

   A. Yes, here is your change.

   B. Sorry, I'm afraid not.

   C. Yes, it's not too far.

5. I'd like to know the interest rate of the dollar.

   A. I can help you.

   B. No, it's not working.

   C. Yes, I'm interested in it.

Duty-free Announcement on Board

Listen to the announcement and fill in the missing words.

Ladies and gentlemen, the duty-free sales will begin **1. shortly**. Please prepare your **2. list** of purchases. Check the Shopping on Board magazine in your seat **3. Pocket**. All prices are in **4. local currency** and in US dollars, and you can pay by cash or by using a credit card. We accept most major credit cards. Frequent flyers win **5. points** on all sales on board. There are some **6. excellent** bargains and there are several items specially designed for our airline.

Dialogue: Price for Items

Listen and tick the price you hear for each item.

Tape scripts

1. Pax: How much is the rose flower perfume?

   CC: That's forty-nine euros, Sir.

   Pax: No, I mean in dollars. How much is it in dollars?

   CC: That's sixty-nine dollars.

   Pax: Can you give me change in dollars?

   CC: I'm afraid I can only give you change in euros, Sir.

2. Pax: Can I see the titanium watch?

   CC: Sure. Here you are. It's eighty-five euros.

   Pax: How much is that in yen?

   CC: Eleven thousand yen, Sir.

3. Pax: I'd like the MP3 player cord, but can I pay in Zloty?

   CC: Yes, Sir.

   Pax: What's twenty-one euros in Zloty?

   CC: It's ninety Zloty.

4. Pax: Can I pay for this pendant with my Visa card?

   CC: Sure.

   Pax: Can you charge in Singapore dollars?

   CC: No problem. It'll be a hundred and twenty Singapore dollars.

5. Pax: Would you mind showing me the designer purse?

   CC: Sure, no problem. That's seventy-nine euros.

   Pax: How much in dirhams?

   CC: Four hundred and twenty-five Dubai dirhams.

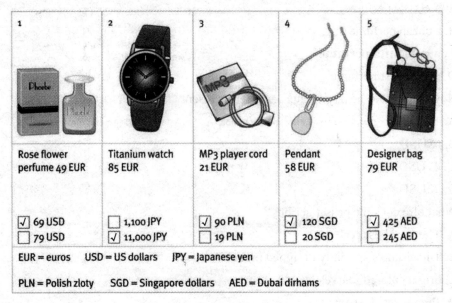

Dialogue: Souvenirs and Gifts on Board

Listen to the following dialogue and choose the proper answer to the question.

Tape scripts

Man: Miss, I'm looking for a light perfume for my daughter's birthday.

FA: I have the perfect one, no .... two. Both are 100 mls. This one is delightful and it's a bargain at only 41 dollars. The other one is a classic --- the very best, but more expensive at 65 dollars.

Man: Which one do you recommend?

FA: I really like this delightful one.

Man: 41 dollars? OK, I'll take it.

FA: How would you like to pay?

Man: By credit card. But just a moment, can I also see the airline's specially designed scarves?

FA: Of course. They're pure silk and they're... let me see, 72 dollars each.

Man: I'll take one.

FA: So that comes to --- let me add it up…41plus72…113 dollars.

Man: OK. Here's my credit card and my frequent flyers card, too, for the points.

FA: Thank you. Would you like a receipt, or just the credit card print-out?

Man: I need the receipt too, please.

FA: No problem. Here's your receipt and your cards and these are your gifts.

Man: Many thanks!

FA: It's a pleasure.

1. What does the passenger want to buy for his daughter?

    A. a classic perfume

    B. a cheap perfume

    C. a delightful perfume

    D. a very best perfume

2. How much does he pay for his daughter's present?

    A. 100USD

    B. 65USD

    C. 41USD

    D. 72USD

3. What else does the passenger buy?

    A. The very best perfume

    B. The airline's specially designed model

    C. bright colored scarves

    D. the pure silk scarves

4. How does he pay for his purchase?

    A. Master card

    B. Frequent flyers miles

    C. Cash

    D. Union pay

5. What does he need with his purchase?

    A. perfume

    B. scarves

    C. Frequent flyers card

    D. The receipt

Keys and Audio scripts

Part III Listening and Understanding

Dialogue: In-flight Sales

Listen to the following dialogue and choose the proper answer to the question.

Tape scripts

CA: Excuse me, sir. Would you like to buy any duty-free items?

P: How much is this box of chocolates?

CA: Godiva chocolate is 3, 100 yen, sir.

P: How much is it in US dollars?

CA: I'll check it for you right away. It's 31 US dollars, sir.

P: Please give me 3 boxes of the Godiva chocolate.

CA: I'm sorry, sir. I'm afraid we have sold out of that item today. This is the only one box. Would you like to see the brand of Ferrero from Italy, very famous and delicious as well. 40 USD for 1 box.

P: All right, I'll take one box of Godiva and 2 boxes of Ferrero. And by the way, I have pre-ordered the aircraft model by the email. Can you help me check?

CA: May I ask if you are a resident of Japan?

P: No.

CA: I am sorry, sir. I'm afraid that is a mail-order item. You need to have an address in Japan to order it, sir.

P: OK, then just those chocolates, please.

1. What item is nearly sold out according to the cabin attendant?

   A. Aircraft model

   B. Ferrero chocolate

   C. no item is sold out.

   D. Godiva chocolate

2. How much of the Godiva chocolate in Japanese yen?

   A. 31

   B. 40

   C. 3100

   D. 71

3. How much totally for all chocolates in USD?

   A. 111

   B. 80

   C. 40

   D. 102

4. What's the requirement to buy the mail-order items?

   A. Must have the airline's member card

   B. Must make the pre-order

   C. Shall be the resident of Japan

   D. All above

5. Which are the final items that the passenger bought?

   A. 3 boxes of Godiva chocolate

   B. 2 boxes of Ferrero and 1 box of Godiva

   C. Aircraft model

   D. All of the items left.

Passage: Some Rules on In-flight Duty-free Purchase in CSA

I. Listen to the following passage and choose the proper answer to the question.

Tape scripts

If your journey with this airline is international, rather than domestic, you will be permitted to buy goods at duty free prices.

Order in-flight:

To order goods available on the return or the next flight, travelers need to fill out the In-flight Order Form in the Guide for duty-free purchase. Certainly, travelers can also make reservations either by telephone, or by visiting online duty-free stores or following the official wechat. Be sure to place an order 48 hours before departure.

Duty-free Allowances:

When travelling abroad, your Duty Free Allowances apply to your country of arrival, not to your country of departure. Your destination country will certainly have different rules and restrictions. Do check your Duty-free Customs Allowances and limits before you travel or consult a flight steward before you buy.

Payment Terms:

A variety of major currencies and credit cards are acceptable to pay for duty-free goods. Each credit card can be used once only in each purchase and the expenditure limit of each person is from $15 to 400 in total.

After-sales Service:

In case of deficiencies or other quality problems with the products you bought on the flight, you can ask for replacement service within 30 days from your purchase, but requests for refunding will not be accepted. All the requests for replacing goods require a complete set of packaging, accessories, gifts, manual, warranty, shopping vouchers,etc. We do not accept products damaged by abuse, misuse, accident or modification.

Keys and Audio scripts

1. Passengers traveling abroad can pre-order duty-free goods in the following ways except _____.

    A. By filling out a personal information form

    B. By making a phone call

    C. By visiting online stores

    D. By following the wechat

2. Which of the following statements is True about the duty-free allowances?

    A. Travelers can buy duty-free goods as much as they can.

    B. Duty-free allowances apply to the country where you buy the products.

    C. Each country has its own rules and restrictions on duty-free allowances.

    D. You'd better travel around the country before you buy .

3. Which of the following statements is not mentioned in the passage?

    A. Credit cards are acceptable to pay for the duty-free goods.

    B. All products sold in flight are marked in CNY.

    C. Each credit card can be used once only in each purchase.

    D. There is the expenditure limit to each person.

4. What would you do in case there is a quality problem with your duty-free product?

    A. Ask flight steward for help.

    B. Require a refund.

    C. Open and use it.

    D. Ask for a replacement.

5. What do you need to require for replacing faulty products?

    A. Packaging and manual.

    B. Accessories and gifts.

    C. Warranty and shopping vouchers.

    D. All of the above.

II. Listen to the following passage again and try to tell whether the following statements are true or not.

1. Passengers are permitted to buy duty-free products in either international or domestic flight. **(F)**

2. Passengers can pre-order the duty-free products by visiting online store at any time. **(F)**

3. When traveling abroad, there is no limit or restriction on what you buy. **(F)**

4. Only RMB and credit cards are acceptable to pay for duty-free goods. **(F)**

5. Passengers need to ask for a replacement for the faulty products within a month since purchase. **(T)**

6. Replacing goods requires shopping vouchers only. **(F)**

95

Part IV Listening and Enjoying

Tape scripts

Star Alliance

Founded in 1997, Star Alliance is the first global airlines alliances. Its headquarters lies in Frankfurt am Main, Germany. Star came from its five original members: Scandinavian Airlines, Thai Airways International, Air Canada, Lufthansa and United Airlines. Now, it has 28 member airlines with more than 1300 airports in 192 countries. Its slogan is "The way the Earth connects".

Star Alliance has two kinds of rewards programs: Silver and Gold based on a customer's status in a member's frequent-flyer program. Codeshare airlines provide passengers with more benefits in flights, desired connections, appropriate ground service, convenient booking, priority boarding and upgrade, infrastructure, communication initiatives and other services. Star Alliance is dedicated to constant innovation in creating and managing products and services that help make the flying experience as comfortable and seamless as possible.

Air China uses Terminal 3E of Beijing Capital International Airport as part of the "Move Under One Roof" program to co-locate alliance members.

I. Listen and choose the right answer to the following questions.

1. How many member airlines are there in Star Alliance?

    A. 197

    B. 28

    C. 1300

    D. 192

2. Which country is not the original member of Star Alliance?

    A. Air China

    B. Lufthansa

    C. United Airlines

    D. Air Canada

3. What benefits can silver passengers have in Star Alliance?

    A. Desired connection

    B. Appropriate ground service

    C. Priority boarding

    D. All of the above

4. Which of the following statements is NOT mentioned?

    A. Star Alliance is based in Germany.

    B. Its slogan is The Way the Earth Connects.

C. Star Alliance takes more market share than other alliances.

D. Air China is a member of "Move Under One Roof" program.

5. What does the word "co-locate" mean here?

   A. Share the same airport

   B. Two airports

   C. Another location

   D. Find a new location

Yoga

II. Listen to the following passage and fill in the missing words.

Tape scripts

Yoga was **originated** in India thousands of years ago. The word "Yoga" means to "yoke" or "unite". Patanjal is often considered the father of yoga and his Yoga-Sutras still strongly influence most styles of modern yoga.

It is a **commonly** misconception that yoga requires people to twist themselves into pretzels or stand on their heads. Not only do you not have to be **flexible** to practise yoga, you also don't need to be young or fit or even ambulatory. In fact, the only requirement for practising yoga is the ability to breathe or meditate.

Regular stretching exercises on strength and patience can improve cardio-pulmonary **function** and coordinate the organism effectively. Yogis try to control themselves by activating potential in their body and stimulating the body's own **natural** healing process.

Yoga now has many different **schools** or styles, all emphasizing the many different aspects of the practice. The top aim is to get spiritual purification through creating a sense of **balance** in the body and mind.

It is quite popular now as a **form** of exercise and relaxation to shape the body and **ease** the stress of modern living. In recent years, an increasing number of scientific studies have measured yoga's effectiveness as a treatment for various ailments, including improving blood pressure, relieving pain, enhancing sleep and boosting **mood**.

Unit 11　Service for Special Passengers

Part I　Pre-listening

Tongue Twisters

Try to read out two or three of the following tongue twisters fluently. Pay attention to your pronunciation.

1. Peter Piper picked a peck of pickled peppers.

A peck of pickled peppers Peter Piper picked.

If Peter Piper picked a peck of pickled peppers,

Where's the peck of pickled peppers Peter Piper picked?

2. The thirty-three thieves thought that they thrilled the throne throughout Thursday.

3. Denise sees the fleece,

   Denise sees the fleas.

   At least Denise could sneeze

   and feed and freeze the fleas.

4. How many boards

   Could the Mongols hoard

   If the Mongol hordes got bored?

5. Send toast to ten tense stout saints' ten tall tents.

6. I saw Susie sitting in a shoe shine shop.

   Where she sits she shines, and where she shines she sits.

7. How can a clam cram in a clean cream can?

Pronunciation

Directions: You'll hear a passage about intonation. Check your understanding of the passage and choose the best answer.

Tape scripts

Language conveys very specific information, such as how to get somewhere or what someone is doing. It can also be used beyond the exact meaning of the words to indicate how the speaker feels about what he is saying, or how he personally feels at that moment.

Generally speaking, if English is not your first language, this is where you start running into difficulty. Even if you pronounce each word clearly, if your intonation patterns are non-standard, your meaning will probably not be clear. Also, in terms of comprehension, you will lose a great deal of information if you are listening only for the actual words used.

This is the starting point of standard intonation. When we say that we need to stress the new information, it's logical to think, "Hmmm, this is the first time I'm saying this sentence, so it's all new information. I'd better stress every word." Well, not quite. In standard English, we consider that the nouns carry the weight of a sentence, when all else is equal. Although the verb carries important information, it does not receive the primary stress of a first-time noun.

1. Language can tell us _____.

   A. How a speaker feels about what he is saying

   B. How a speaker feels at the moment he is speaking

   C. Both of the above

2. If your intonation patterns are not standard, _____.

   A. everyone will understand you

Keys and Audio scripts

    B. your meaning will probably not be clear

    C. neither of the above

3. What is usually stressed in a sentence?

    A. Every word

    B. Nouns

    C. Pronouns

4. After the nouns have been introduced and we begin using pronouns, which words are usually stressed?

    A. Verbs

    B. Pronouns

    C. Adjectives

Intonation

Directions: Listen and try to read the following sentences. Pay attention to the intonation.

Falling Intonation

◎ Where's the nearest p↘ost-office?

◎ What time does the film f↘inish?

◎ I think we are completely l↘ost.

◎ OK, here's the magaz↘ine you wanted.

Rising Intonation

◎ I hear the Health Centre is expanding. So, is that the new d↗octor?

◎ Are you th↗irsty?

Fall-rise Intonation

◎ I do↘n't support any football team at the m↘om↗ent. (but I may change my mind in the future).

◎ It rained every day in the firs↘t w↗eek. (but things improved after that).

◎ Is this your cam↘er↗a?

◎ Would you like another co↘ff↗ee?

Think and try to read out the following announcements. Pay attention to your intonation.

1. There are eight (ten) emergency exits / located at the forward↗, rear↗ and middle↘.

2. We would ask you to ensure that (the window shade is open)↗, (your seatbelt fastened)↗, (your tray table stowed)↗ and (your seatback brought to the upright position)↘.

Part II   Listening In

Responses

You will hear five sentences. Listen carefully and select the best response to each question or statement.

1. Are there any unaccompanied children in today's flight?

    A. She is ten years old.

    B. How old is she?

    C. Yes. There are two.

2. Can I apply for wheelchair services?

    A. Have a nice trip.

    B. Please fill in this form.

    C. I don't know.

3. May I help you with your infant?

    A. Sorry, I won't.

    B. Thank you.

    C. It doesn't matter.

4. How long have you been pregnant?

    A. It's a boy.

    B. Five months.

    C. I'm not comfortable..

5. What's the date today?

    A. It's Tuesday.

    B. It's April the 20th.

    C. It's a good day.

Dialogue: Service for Special Passengers

    Linda works as a flight attendant in the Sky Airlines. Today her flight is from Tokyo to Hong Kong. There are several special passengers in today's flight. Listen carefully and fill in the missing information please.

Tape scripts

    1. Cabin Crew: Hi, little boy. Are you Tomas Anderson? Do you have a nick name? May I call you Tommy?

    Passenger: Yes. I am Tommy.

    Cabin Crew: I'll take you to your seat. Please let us know if you need any help.

    Passenger: Thank you.

    Cabin Crew: Here's your seat. Sit down please and I'll help you fasten your seatbelt. I'll keep your traveling documents and return ticket, then I will give it to the ground staff when you leave the plane.

    2. Cabin Crew: Good morning, Ms. Smith. May I help with your hand luggage?

    Passenger: Yes. Thank you. I am pregnant, and I'm a little nervous. Do you have an air sickness bag on the flight?

    Cabin Crew: I hope you can relax. I will help adjust the seatback and air vent for you. An air sickness bag is in the seat pocket in front of you. I'll be right back with a hot towel and water.

Passenger: Thank you. I feel better now.

3. Cabin Crew: Good morning, are you Mr. Merman? May I help you with your baggage?

Passenger: Yes. I'm Richard Merman.

Cabin Crew: Would you mind holding my arm? I will take you to your seat if you like.

Passenger: Thanks.

Cabin Crew: Mr. Merman, I'll introduce the meal for you. Imagine the tray set is like a clock: salad is at 12 o'clock and entrée is at 6 o'clock. Please be careful because the entree is very hot.

Passenger: Okay. Thank you for your patience.

4. Passenger: Do you have bassinet on board?

Cabin Crew: I'm sorry, Ms. Diana. There is no bassinet on board, but I will try to find some vacant seat, and lift up the armrest for your baby to lie down.

Passenger: Thank you.

Cabin Crew: Excuse me, Ms. Dianna. The aircraft will be taking off. Let me help you to fasten the seatbelt for your infant.

Passenger: Okay. Thanks.

Name	Special Passenger	Matters Need Attention
Tomas Anderson	unaccompanied **Child**	• take him to his **seat** • help him fasten his **seatbelt** • keeping his **traveling** documents and return ticket
Ms. Smith	pregnant	• She has been pregnant about **21** weeks. • help adjust the **seatback** and air vent • an **air sickness bag** is in the seat pocket • provide with a **hot towel** and water
Richard Merman	blind passenger	• help with his **baggage** • take him to his seat if he likes • introduce the meal: the tray set is like **a clock**
Dianna	passenger with a **baby**	• there is no **bassinet** on board • try to find some **vacant** seat • lift up the **armrest** for the baby to lie down • help to fasten the **infant** seatbelt

Dialogue: Check-in for Special Passengers

I. Listen to the following dialogue and choose the proper answer to the question.

Tape scripts

Airport staff: Good morning, ma'am.

Passenger 1: Good morning.

Airport staff: Just yourself, ma'am?

Passenger 1: No. I'm here for my brother. He is disabled and needs special assistance.

Airport staff: That won't be a problem, ma'am. May I have his ticket and passport, please?

Passenger 1: Here you are.

Airport staff: Ma'am, here is a form, please fill in the form with details, such as personal information, situation of an illness and special needs. Especially, please read the exceptions clause carefully and sign here.

Passenger 1: No problem.

Airport Staff: Thank you. How many bags is the gentleman checking in?

Passenger 1: He's not checking any bags. He just has a carry onbag.

Airport Staff: He will be seated on the 1st row. According to our regulations, he needs to use our wheelchair and check his in.

Passenger 1: Ok, I'll check it.

Airport Staff: Our stuff will bring him down to the gate. He then will be lifted onto the plane, and our stuff will help him off as well. Here is his boarding pass and passport. Please wait on the side.

Passenger 1: Thanks a lot.

Airport Staff: My pleasure. Next one, please. Good morning, may I see your passport?

Passenger 2: I'm checking in for my daughter.

Airport staff: Okay. How old is she?

Passenger 2: She is 11 years old.

Airport Staff: I see. Could you fill this form with details, such as contact number, address, where she is traveling, and the details of the person who is going to pick her at the destination airport?

Passenger 2: Okay, thanks.

1. How many special passengers are mentioned in this dialogue?

   A. One

   B. Two

   C. Three

   D. Four

2. How many bags are the gentleman checking in?

   A. Only one piece of baggage.

   B. Two pieces of baggage.

   C. Three pieces of baggage.

   D. He's not checking any.

3. How old is the child?

   A. 9 years old

   B. 10 years old

   C. 11 years old

   D. 12 years old

4. What information is not mentioned in the form of disabled passenger?

   A. Personal information

   B. Situation of an illness

   C. Where he is traveling to

   D. Exceptions clause

5. What information is not mentioned in the form of Unaccompanied Children?

   A. Telephone number

   B. Destination

   C. Special needs

   D. Address

II. Listen to the dialogue again and try to tell whether the following statements are true or not.

1. The lady here is checking in for her husband. **(F)**
2. The lady has to read the exceptions clause carefully and sign. **(T)**
3. The disabled gentleman needn't check in his wheelchair. **(F)**
4. The disabled gentleman's seat is in the last row. **(F)**
5. If you check in for an unaccompanied child, you will fill in a form. **(T)**

Dialogue: Passenger with an Infant

Listen carefully to the following interview and try to find out the proper answers.

Tape scripts

Cabin Crew: Good afternoon, ma'am.

Passenger: Good afternoon, could you please help me put my baby stroller somewhere?

Cabin Crew: Sorry. Your stroller has to be checked in.

Passenger: Oh, then how can I get it back? I'll need it when getting off the plane.

Cabin Crew: When we arrive at San Francisco, we'll ask the ground staff to pick your stroller in advance and bring it at the cabin door for you. We'll inform you when it is ready. Would that be okay?

Passenger: Okay. Thanks a lot. Excuse me, can you help me make a bottle of milk for my daughter?

Cabin Crew: Sure. How much water do you need?

Passenger: Give me some warm water. Check the scale on the bottle, I need about 180ml of water. Then scoop up six spoons of milk powder and add them into the water.

Cabin Crew: Sure. Wait a minute, ma'am.

Passenger: Thanks. By the way, my daughter has been crying when the aircraft is taking off. Is there something wrong?

Cabin Crew: Don't worry. Maybe her ears can feel the uncomfortable pressure while taking off. This is normal.

Passenger: I hope so. Thank you.

1. Could the passenger's stroller be put in the cabin?

    A. Yes.

    B. No.

    C. Yes, but she needs to go through the security check.

    D. Not mentioned.

2. Where is the passenger's destination?

    A. Peking.

    B. New York.

    C. San Francisco.

    D. Hong Kong.

3. Who will pick up the stroller in advance and bring it at the cabin door?

    A. The flight attendant.

    B. The captain.

    C. The ground staff.

    D. The passenger's husband.

4. How many spoons of milk powder does the passenger need for her daughter?

    A. Three

    B. Five

    C. Six

    D. Eight

5. Why is the baby crying?

    A. She may feel the uncomfortable pressure.

    B. She is ill.

    C. She's hungry.

    D. She needs her mother.

Part III   Listening and Understanding

Dialogue: Upgrading

Number the sentences in the correct order according to the dialogue.

Tape scripts

Airlines Staff: Excuse me, sir. Is there anything I can do for you?

Passenger: Here is my Silver Card. May I have an upgrade?

Airlines Staff: I am sorry, sir. Our first class is fully booked today. We are unable to offer you such a seat today.

Passenger: Ok. It doesn't matter. But is there any vacant seat in the front of the cabin? The middle seat is too narrow and it makes me uncomfortable.

Airlines staff: Wait a minute, I'll check it. Excuse me, sir. There are only front window seats now. Would you like it?

Passengers: That's okay. Thank you.

3〇 Our first class is fully booked today.
7〇 That's okay. Thank you.
4〇 We are unable to offer you such a seat today.
6〇 There are only front window seats now.
1〇 Is there anything I can do for you?
5〇 The middle seat is too narrow and it makes me uncomfortable.
2〇 May I have an upgrade?

Passage: Assistance for Incapacitated Passengers

Listen to the passage and fill in the missing words.

Tape scripts

Incapacitated passengers are those who, because of their medical, **physical** or mental condition, require individual attention which is not normally provided to other passengers. This attention may be required on **embarking**, disembarking, in-flight, in an **emergency evacuation** or during ground handling.

Some incapacitated passengers may have **permanent** but stable disabilities, such as arthritis, deafness, **blindness**, or paralysis of all or part of the body. Others may **have temporary disabilities such as recent surgery**, **broken limbs**, **or recent illness** which requires them to be on a stretcher or in a **wheelchair**.

Not all incapacitated passengers require medical **clearance** before being accepted for travel. However, passengers with the following incapacities or disabilities must be **subject to** medical clearance by our Medical Services Department before being accepted for travel.

If you have enquiries **regarding** the assistance provided for specific conditions, please call our customer care center at 503 4798 5000.

Part IV Listening and Enjoying

Some Famous Airports in the World

I. Listen to the following passage and choose the proper answer to the question.

Tape scripts

There are many airports in the world. This is partly because of the popularity of air travel and the lower budget flights availability which has caused an expansion in the number of airports. Here we are going to introduce some world famous international airports.

Heathrow Airport is currently the busiest airport in the UK and serves passengers for domestic flights within the UK, external flights to the rest of the world and it is also a hub for connecting flights to many countries as well.

  Beijing Capital International Airport is one of the world's busiest airport and one of the largest Chinese airports. It is located 32 km (20 miles) northeast of city center, at Chaoyang-Shunyi District. Beijing Airport is a hub for Air China, China Eastern Airlines, China Southern Airlines, Hainan Airlines, and a Focus city for Sichuan Airlines, Shenzhen Airlines and Shandong Airlines.

  The Dubai International Airport is one of the world's busiest airport located in Dubai, United Arab Emirates. It is considered the busiest airport operation through only two runways, the third-busiest airport in the world by passenger traffic, the sixth-busiest cargo airport in the world.

  Seoul Airport, known officially as Incheon International Airport, is the largest airport in South Korea. The airport operates as a hub for cargo traffic and international civilian air transportation in East Asia. Most of the flights operated at Incheon Airport are domestic and shuttle flights that alternate the airports in Taiwan, China and Japan.

  1. How many airports are mentioned in the passage?

   A. 2

   B. 3

   C. 4

   D. 5

  2. Where is Heathrow International Airport?

   A. The United States

   B. The United Kingdom

   C. Japan

   D. Saudi Arabia

  3. Which airport is the third-busiest airport in the world by passenger traffic?

   A. Heathrow International Airport

   B. Beijing Capital International Airport

   C. Incheon International Airport

   D. Dubai International Airport

  4. Which airport operates as a hub for cargo traffic and international civilian air transportation in East Asia?

   A. Heathrow International Airport

   B. Beijing Capital International Airport

   C. Incheon International Airport

   D. Dubai International Airport

  5. Beijing Airport is not a hub for _____.

   A. Air China

   B. China Southern Airlines

Keys and Audio scripts

   C. Shandong Airlines
   D. Xiamen Airlines
II. Enjoy the song and complete the missing lyrics.

Winter in My Heart

Winter has come
farewell to the sun
it's getting colder every **single** day

you are not here
can't stand you're not near
I'll wait for you forever and I pray
my **fantasy** makes me believe that you're with me

I have winter in my heart
cause I miss you more than **words** can say
when nights are long and **lonely** without you

I have winter in my heart
count the hours every single day
that **lonesome** time is too sad to be true
got winter in my heart

snow **falling** down
and you're not around
I'm all alone in that white **wonderland**
taking a walk
there's no one to **talk**
we used to be **together** hand in hand
my fantasy makes me believe that you're with me

I have winter in my heart
cause I miss you more than words can say
when nights are long and lonely without you
I have winter in my heart
count the hours every single day
that lonesome time is too sad to be true
got winter in my heart

Unit 12　Emergency Situations

Part I　Pre-listening

Slangs

Complete the following sentences and then try to find out the meanings of the slangs about "fish".

1. Mr. Smith looks like a **cold** fish.

"A cold fish" means a cold person.

2. I can't believe it! His only daughter was hurt in an **accident** and he didn't go to the hospital just because he had other fish to **fry** ——a million-dollar deal he was closing.

"Have other fish to fry" means to have got something more important to do.

3. Never **offer** to teach fish to swim.

"teach fish to swim" means to teach or show somebody with what they are good at.

4. In her hometown, she was a big fish in a small **pond**, but after then moved to New York, she was just only one among many millions.

"a big fish" means an important person.

5. It's like **shooting** fish in a barrel.

"shooting fish in a barrel" means a piece of cake; very easy

Pronunciation

I. Read the following paragraph and mark the sense groups with "/".

College students can get an assistance/ from the government /when they can not afford their tuition fee. Eligible students can be granted/ with an unequal amount /including living cost /according to their family status. Otherwise, students may choose to/ apply to the Students Loans Company /for a student loan/ with low interest rate. Loans are supposed to be repaid /after they graduate /and get a job.

II. Answer the questions according to what you hear.

1. Who?　　　　　**A first-class passenger** is asking for a blanket.
2. Where?　　　　Henry's flight to Bangkok will get aboard at **Gate 19**.
3. What?　　　　 She is **making landing announcement**.
4. How?　　　　　Mr. and Mrs. White like travelling **by train**.
5. How long?　　　It takes **7 hours or so** to get to Sydney.
6. Why?　　　　　The flight to Xiamen has been cancelled because of **the storm**.
7. How much?　　The fare to Guangzhou is discounted to **900 yuan**.
8. How often?　　 The airport shuttle leaves **every 15 minutes**.

Keys and Audio scripts

9. When? The passengers to Paris are going to board **10 minutes later**.
10. Whom? Steve is talking with **a blond girl** over there.

Part II Listening In

Responses

You will hear five sentences. Listen carefully and select the best response to each question or statement.

1. Would you please help me with the earphone?
   A. Yes, my pleasure.
   B. That won't help.
   C. It's near the airport.

2. Do you know why the plane is delayed?
   A. Yes, the plane is delayed.
   B. I'm playing the piano.
   C. It's the storm.

3. What time does the plane arrive from Boston?
   A. It takes about 5 hours.
   B. I don't like a morning flight.
   C. Let me ask the stuff here.

4. Would you rather have cream and sugar with your coffee?
   A. Neither, please.
   B. Help yourself, please.
   C. The ice cream is melted.

5. Mr. Bush is responsible for the flight, isn't he?
   A. Don't push the button.
   B. Ask the Purser to make sure.
   C. Yes, it's alright.

Dialogues: Medical Problems

Listen and match each conversation with a medical problem.

Tape scripts

1. Pax: OUCH! OW, OW, OW!
   CC: I'll get the bag! Are you all right, sir?
   Pax: I opened the locker, and that bag hit me in the head!
   CC: Oh, no! Here, sit down. Let's move the bag.
   Pax: OK.
   CC: You need to put something on that cut. I'll get a band aid for you.

2. Pax: Er, excuse me.

109

CC: Yes, sir. Can I help?

Pax: My nose. It's bleeding.

CC: Here, take these tissues, that's it....I suggest you sit upright and lean forward slightly. Don't put your head back.

Pax: Thanks.

CC: No worries. If I were you, I'd put the sick bag on your lap. Just let any blood run into it. I'll just get some more tissues, and some ice. Are you OK for a minute?

Pax: Uh-huh.

3. Pax 1: Mum! My ears hurt!!

Pax 2: I know, I know. Just try swallowing. That'll help.

Pax 1: I can't. They hurt.. My ears hurt! Make it stop!

CC: Shall I help? How about sucking one of these sweets? I think you should have one--it can really help to stop the pain.

Pax 1: Thanks.

CC: No problem.

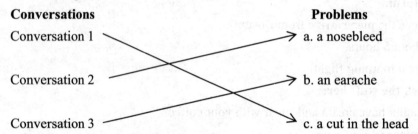

Announcement: Sudden Emergency Announcement

Try to fill in the missing words of the following sudden announcement from the purser. Then listen and check your answers.

Ladies and gentlemen, this is an **1. emergency**. This is an emergency. **2. Stay** in your seats with your seat belts **3. fastened**. Remain **4. calm** and **5. follow** these instructions. Pull down the oxygen mask. Pull down the oxygen mask. Put it **6. over** your nose and **7. mouth** immediately and breathe **8. normally**. Adjust the **9. band** to secure it. Do make sure your own mask is fitted properly **10. before** helping anyone else.

Dialogue: The Injured Passenger on Board

Listen carefully and choose the proper answer to the question.

Tape scripts

Leila: Is she travelling with you, sir?

Man: No, I think she's alone. I haven't spoken to her, but I don't think she's travelling with anyone.

Leila: Hello, hello. How are you feeling?

Woman: Oh. Everything just went black.

Keys and Audio scripts

Leila: Do you have any pain?

Woman: I'm a bit dizzy, that's all.

Leila: You've had a nasty bang on your head. How are you feeling?

Woman: Not too bad.

Leila: Would you like a glass of water?

Woman: Yes, that would be good.

Leila: You've got a small cut on your forehead. It doesn't look too serious, though, I'm going to clean up the wound and put a dressing over it.

Woman: I'm better now. Thank you very much.

Leila: I'm glad you're feeling all right. Can you hold this compress against your forehead? The captain has switched on the seatbelts sign, so if you feel able to sit up, I could help you with your seatbelt. I'll come back and check on you in a few moments.

1. Who is the injured passenger traveling with?

   A. With her husband

   B. The man who just went back

   C. With a woman

   D. Nobody

2. What happened to the injured passenger?

   A. She got a crash on her forehead when turbulence.

   B. She had a nasty bang on her head.

   C. She was fine without any bad feeling.

   D. She got a headache on board.

3. How did the cabin crew deal with the injured passenger?

   A. They didn't use the first aid kit.

   B. Leila helped clean up the wound and put a dressing over it.

   C. Leila got the passenger a glass of water.

   D. They didn't take any action to deal with the wound, only asked the passenger's feeling.

4. What did Leila want the injured passenger to do?

   A. Take some medicine

   B. Go to have a seat

   C. compress against the forehead

   D. Both B and C

Dialogue: Is there a Doctor on Board?

Listen to the dialogue and try to tell whether the following statements are true or not.

Tape scripts

Woman: Help! Help! My husband's unconscious.

111

Rani: OK, where is he? Bill, grab the oxygen and a defibrillator from the medial kit and call Anton of a medical emergency.

Bill: OK.

[Short pause]

Rani: Hello, can you hear me? [to his wife:] Are you travelling with this passenger?

Woman: I'm his wife. He said he had a bit of indigestion - that was all. He stood up to go to the toilet and then he collapsed.

Rani: He's very grey. He's not breathing. Let's get him on the floor now. ... Oh, he's breathing again. [to wife] Has this ever happened before?

Woman: Not as far as I know.

Rani: Bill, help me get the mask over his head.

Doctor: I'm a doctor, what's the problem?

Woman: Oh, thank goodness.

Rani: Hello doctor, thank you for coming. This passenger is unconscious and he stopped breathing for a few seconds. We administered CPR for two minutes and he's breathing again, although his pulse is very weak and his breathing is shallow. We're just administering oxygen ...

Doctor: OK Madam, How old is he? Is he on any medication?

Woman: Sixty-three. He's a diabetic. So he has injections for that.

Doctor: And in good health usually?

Woman Yes, but he's been very tired recently. Is he going to be all right?

Rani: Don't worry. We're taking care of him.

1. The sick passenger is unconscious. **(T)**

2. The sick passenger is travelling alone. **(F)**

3. The sick passenger is 73 years old. **(F)**

4. Rani needs help from other passengers, so he ask them to stay around the sick passenger. **(F)**

5. Rani wants to put the sick passenger in a seat. **(F)**

6. The sick passenger had collapsed before. **(F)**

7. Rani and Bill give the sick passenger oxygen. **(T)**

8. Rani and Bill can deal with the situation themselves. **(F)**

9. The sick passenger is on medication. **(T)**

10. The sick passenger is in good health. **(F)**

11. Sarah tells Anton, the purser, about the situation. **(F)**

12. There isn't a doctor on board. **(F)**

Part III Listening and Understanding

Dialogue: Emergency commands

Choose the emergency command to match the emergency situation according to what you hear.

Tape scripts

Instructor: Good morning, everyone. Today, let's review the emergency evacuation commands. It's the cabin crew's response to evacuate from the aircraft, giving clear direction is critical in directing a successful evacuation. The evacuation commands must be: continuous, positive, concise, motivating, loud and strong.

Situation 1: Bracing commands, in an unanticipated emergency: at the point of impact, what's the commands?

Trainee: Grab ankles! Head Down! Stay low!

Instructor: Good, then how about in an anticipated emergency command?

Trainee: Upon hearing the bracing signal or the point of impact yell commands: Brace!

Instructor: Super, next.

Situation 2: What's the Evacuation commands of the ditching situation to evacuate?

Trainee: Release seat belts! Get your life vest! Get up! Get out!

Instructor: All right, then in the emergency landing, how to command the first two able-bodied passengers evacuating?

Trainee: You two, Stay at the bottom! Help people off!

Instructor: If in the ditching situation, how to instruct passenger to go off the front of the wing?

Trainee: Inflate your life vest! Step through! Turn. Go off the front of the wing!

Instructor: That's it. Let's finish this test. Once again, please be aware that the evacuation commands must be: continuous, positive, concise, motivating, loud and strong. Now have a short break.

Emergency Situations

1. Bracing commands, in an unanticipated emergency   B
2. Bracing commands, in an anticipated emergency command   C
3. The Evacuation commands of the ditching situation to evacuate   E
4. In the emergency landing, command the first two able-bodied passengers evacuating   D
5. In the ditching situation, instruct passenger to go off the front of the wing.   A

Emergency Commands

A. Inflate your life vest! Step through! Turn .Go off the front of the wing!

B. Grab ankles! Head Down! Stay low!

C. Brace!

D. You two, Stay at the bottom! Help people off!

E. Release seat belts! Get your life vest! Get up! Get out!

Announcement: Preparing for an Emergency Evacuation

I. Listen to the following dialogue and choose the proper answer to the question.

Tape scripts

Captain: Ladies and gentlemen, your captain speaking. We have a technical problem and for everyone's safety we've decided to land in the next 20 minutes at the nearest airport. The landing should be perfectly normal but for safety reasons we will evacuate the aircraft using the slides. The cabin crew will now give you full instructions and prepare you for the landing. Please listen carefully to their instructions. Thank you.

Purser: Ladies and gentlemen. This is purser speaking. Please return to your seats immediately and keep your seatbelt fastened securely.

We are now going to take you through our safety procedures. Please watch and listen carefully. The safety card in your seat pocket shows details of your escape routes, oxygen masks and life jackets. It also shows the bracing position which you must adopt in an emergency landing. Again, please listen carefully. Emergency exits are on both sides of the aircraft. They are clearly marked and are being pointed out to you now.

On the main deck there are two exits at the rear of the First-class cabin and two at the front and rear of each other cabin section. On the upper deck there is an emergency exit on each side, in the middle of the cabin. Please take a moment now to locate the exit nearest to you.

Do not leave your seats until instructed to do so by your crew. When the seatbelt signs are switched off, make your way to your nearest exit. Leave all personal belongings behind. I repeat, leave all personal hand baggage behind. Ladies, remove high-heeled shoes, as they may tear the slide.

1. According to the captain's announcement, what will they use to evacuate from the aircraft?

    A. lift raft

    B. escape routes

    C. evacuation slide

    D. oxygen masks

2. What does the purser not mention about the safety procedures?

    A. safety card

    B. life jackets.

    C. Emergency exits

    D. flashing light

3. How many emergency exits are on the upper deck?

    A. 2

B. 5
C. 8
D. 6

4. Which of the following statements is correct?
   A. Passengers can evacuate with all personal belongings.
   B. This emergency Evacuation will be dangerous if passenger don't follow the commands.
   C. The safety card in your overhead compartment shows details of your escape routes, oxygen masks and life jackets.
   D. passengers must remain seated and follow instructions by captain.

II. Listen to the dialogue again and try to tell whether the following statements are true or not.

1. The reason that the captain decided to emergency landing was the abnormal aircraft altitude. **(F)**
2. Captain decided to land in the next 20 minutes at the nearest airport. **(T)**
3. The first command from the purser was the passengers must return to seat immediately and fasten seatbelt. **(T)**
4. Use the furthest exit to evacuate. **(F)**
5. It's forbidden to bring everything when evacuating. **(T)**
6. Passengers can evacuate with high-heeled shoes. **(F)**
7. When the seatbelt signs are switched off, passengers can run. **(F)**

Part IV   Listening and Enjoying

Passage: Film on Pilot's Heroic Story to Begin Shooting

Number the sentences in the correct order according to the passage.

Tape scripts

The heroic deeds of Liu Chuanjian, a Chinese pilot who was applauded after successfully handling an emergency landing, will hit screens in China.

Popular actor Zhang Hanyu will feature in the movie to be directed by Liu Weiqiang. The film will see start shooting in January and is expected to hit screens within 2019.

The story is based on the real experience of Liu Chuanjian, a Sichuan Airlines' captain who in May 2018 calmly landed a flight after a 20-minute struggle with the loss of cabin pressure. He was operating the Airbus A319 from Chongqing to Lhasa, Tibet, when a windshield suddenly broke at 32,000 feet above the ground and his co-pilot was sucked halfway out of the window and was saved by the seat belt. Liu landed the plane safely with none of the passengers was injured.

Liu was honored with five million yuan ($730,000) and hailed the "hero captain of China's civil aviation". He told the media later that he was confident at the time that he could steer the plane to the nearest airport manually when the automatic systems stopped working.

1○ Liu Chuanjian, a Sichuan Airlines' captain.

7○ Therefore, after successfully handling an emergency landing, the captain Liu and his heroic story will hit screens in China.

8○ Popular actor Zhang Hanyu will feature in the movie to be directed by Liu Weiqiang. The film will see start shooting in January and is expected to hit screens within 2019.

3○ At that time, he was operating the Airbus A319 from Chongqing to Lhasa, Tibet.

6○ Liu was honored with five million yuan ($730,000) prize and hailed the "hero captain of China's civil aviation".

4○ A windshield suddenly broke at 32,000 feet above the ground and his co-pilot was sucked halfway out of the window and was saved by the seat belt.

2○ In May 2018, he calmly landed a flight after a 20-minute struggle with the loss of cabin pressure.

5○ Liu landed the plane safely with none of the passengers injured.

Culture Perspective: Tennis Tournaments

Choose the words you hear to fill in the blanks.

Tape scripts

Court tennis is also known as royal tennis. It **originated** in France during the Middle Ages. It is a tradition that players must be dressed in white sportswear. In 1884, Wimbledon inaugurated a women's **championship**.

There are four major tennis **tournaments** in the world. Wimbledon is **considered** as the oldest and the most important one. It is held in **late** June and early July every year. Unlike Wimbledon which is played on grass, the US Open, the French Open and the Australia Open are played on clay or hard **courts**. "Open" originally meant that any players can take part in the competition if they want. But now, only players with certain rank can be **qualified** for the competition. Among the four tournaments, the Us Open offers the most prize money.

Winning all four in the same year is called a grand slam. Don Budge was the first winner of the **Grand** Slam tournaments in 1938.

ITF (The International Tennis Federation) is the governing **body** of world tennis, wheelchair tennis, and beach tennis. It was founded in 1913 by twelve national **associations** and as of 2016, is affiliated with 211 national tennis associations and six regional associations. The ITF's governance responsibilities include maintaining and **enforcing** the rules of tennis, regulating international team competitions, **promoting** the game, and preserving the sport's integrity via anti-doping and anti-corruption programs.

Unit 13 Transfer Service

Part I Pre-listening

Opposites: Try to write down the opposites of the following words.

1. Light —— __heavy__
2. Major —— __minor__
3. Coward —— __brave__
4. Safe —— __dangerous__
5. Deep —— __shallow__
6. Exit —— __entrance__

Pronunciation

I. Write down the names of cities or countries you hear.

Tape scripts

1. Egypt is one of the four ancient civilizations.
2. Brazil is called "a Football Kingdom".
3. Chicago is an important hub in the north of the United States.
4. Toronto is one of the most livable cities in the world.
5. Indians like cooking with curry.
6. Is Sydney the capital of Australia?
7. Many international conferences are held in Brussels every year.
8. Vienna is world-famous for classic music and great musicians.

	Country	Capital	City	Language or people
1	**Egypt**	Cairo	e.g. Suez	Egyptian
2	**Brazil**	Brasilia	e.g. St. Paul	Brazilian
3	The United States	Washington DC	e.g. **Chicago**	American
4	Canada	Ottawa	e.g. **Toronto**	Canadian
5	India	New Deli	e.g. Bombay	**Indian**
6	Australia	Canberra	e.g. **Sydney**	Australian
7	Switzerland	Berne	e.g. **Brussels**	Swiss
8	Austria	**Vienna**	e.g. Innsbruck	Austrian

II. Complete this part as well as you possibly can.

Tape scripts

Schedule

Dr. Harrison is going to Rome on business. Please complete his timetable according to what

117

you hear.

Steve: Hello, Dr. Harrison. This is Steve Claire from Paris Company.

Dr. Harrison: Oh, hello Steve. How are you?

Steve: Fine, thank you. I'm calling to arrange a meeting with you next week.

Dr. Harrison: When would you be available?

Steve: Are you free on Wednesday afternoon?

Dr. Harrison: Let me see. I'm going to have lunch with Mr. Albert at 12:10. And then I have an appointment with an agent.

Steve: How about the 23rd?

Dr. Harrison: I'll attend the fair all day on Thursday. What about Friday morning? Is 9 o'clock ok?

Steve: That would be fine. By the way, what flight are you going to take? I'll pick you up at the airport.

Dr. Harrison: It's flight AZ651. Thank you very much. See you then.

March			
21st	Tuesday	10:10 a.m.	Flight **AZ651** to Paris
		18:30 p.m.	dinner with Mr. Morris
22nd	**Wednesday**	9:30 a.m.	visit new factory
		12:10 p.m.	lunch with Ms. Albert
		14:30 p.m.	**appointment with an agent**
23rd	Thursday	all day	attend the fair
24th	Friday	9:00 a.m.	**meet with Steve**
		15:50 p.m	Flight 652 back

Part II   Listening In

Responses

You will hear five sentences. Listen carefully and select the best response to the question or statement.

1. Where can I get a blanket?

   A. Ask the stewardess for it.

   B. Yes, there is a blanket.

   C. Don't forget to take it.

2. When does the express delivery arrive from Shenzhen?

   A. By air mail.

   B. Yes, it arrived on time.

   C. In 3 days or so.

3. I can't find the transfer counter.

   A. Let me show you.

   B. Yes, I need your help.

   C. You can open another account.

4. I'm not completely satisfied with your customer service.

   A. It's good to me.

   B. No, it's not completed.

   C. I'm sorry to hear that. What can I help you with?

5. What plane are you catching to Madrid?

   A. I plan to get there by air.

   B. You can board now.

   C. A non-stop flight.

Dialogue: My Luggage in Connecting Flight

Listen to the following dialogue and choose the proper answer to the question,

Tape scripts

C: Good afternoon, sir. Is there anything I can help you with?

P: Well, my flight has just landed from Bangkok and I'm going to take another flight to Rome in three hours. I'm wondering whether I've got to go through immigration and check in my baggage.

C: If your connecting flight is operated by a Star Alliance member airline, you can check your bags through to the final destination. What flight are you traveling on?

P: AMS, I think. Is it one of your partner airlines?

C: Yes, it is. So you don't bother to clear customs and check in again.

P: That would be fine. What a relief!

C: But I'm afraid you have to board in another terminal.

P: How can I get there, then?

C: You can take the airport transfer shuttle train over there. It's fast and convenient.

P: Thank you very much.

C: It's my pleasure. Enjoy your trip!

1. Where does the man want to go?

   A. Home

   B. Italy

   C. Bangkok

   D. California

2. What flight is the man traveling with?

   A. Bangkok airline

B. A partner

C. A member airline of Star Alliance

D. Immigration officer

3. Does the man have to check in again?

A. Yes, he does.

B. No, he doesn't

C. Yes, he has to check through the immigration.

D. No, he doesn't have to be relief.

4. How can he get to the terminal?

A. Walk on foot.

B. Take the bus

C. Take the shuttle train

D. Take the subway

Passage: Why Book Your Airport Transfer with Us?

Listen to the following passage and fill in the missing words.

Tape scripts

Conxxe is a worldwide transport service, offering you airport to city and 1) <u>resort</u> transfers in over 21,000 destinations in over 150 countries around the world.

• Comfortable transport from/to airports

Wide range of safe & licensed 2) <u>vehicles</u>, including cars, shared shuttles & chauffeured limousines

• Outstanding value & quality service

• Fully inclusive 3) <u>pricing</u>, no 4) <u>hidden</u> extras

• Pre-book online and avoid queues for a hassle free arrival

• 22,000+ positive independent customer 5) <u>reviews</u>

• 24/7 service and support helpline, emergency cover gives peace of mind

• $20 transit 6) <u>voucher</u> is valid from now till September 30, 2020 to offset your 7) <u>outlet</u> shopping and dinning during your transit at our airport. The transit voucher can also be redeemed for one-time access to the Ambassador Lounge at 8) <u>Terminals</u> 2 or 3 for up to two hours; as well as selected spa and massage services at Spa Express in Terminal 2. The Ambassador 9) <u>Lounge</u> provides shower facilities (including basic toiletries), 10) <u>light</u> refreshments, reading material and complimentary WiFi.

Dialogue: Free Singapore Bus Tour During Your Transit

I. Listen to the following dialogue and choose the proper answer to each question.

Tape scripts

A: Good morning, madam. What can I do for you?

Keys and Audio scripts

P: Good morning. I've got about seven hours before I connect my next flight, so I'd like to have a look around the city during my stopover . What would you recommend?

A: There is a Free Singapore Bus Tour open to all passengers transiting in Changi Airport.

P: That sounds wonderful!

A: Yes, it really is. There are two different tour routes: Heritage Tour and City Sights Tour.

P: Which one is better?

A: Well, Heritage tour is truly a sight. Historical monuments like the city hall, are littered throughout the colonial district. A stark contrasts to the modern skyscrapers, the national monuments have withstood decades of Singapore's history.

P: So I can visit Singapore's national icon the Merlion in this route?

A: That's right.

P: OK, great! What about the other route?

A: City Sights Tour will offer you a panoramic night view of Singapore's famous icons along the Marina Bay – the Singapore Flyer, Marina Bay Sands, the Esplanade and Gardens by the Bay.

P: I can't wait to see.

A: Each tour is 2.5 hours long. You can choose both of the two routes since your transit is more than 5.5 hours. And here is your brochure. You can find more details.

P: Thank you so much.

A: Have a nice day!

1. How long will the woman stay in Singapore?

   A. 2.5 hours

   B. More than 5.5 hours

   C. Less than 5.5 hours

   D. Two days

2. Which of the following statements about Heritage Tour is true?

   A. Heritage Tour is to visit modern skyscrapers.

   B. Heritage Tour is better than City Sights Tour.

   C. There are quiet a few of historical monuments.

   D. The woman doesn't like Heritage Tour.

3. Which of the following place is not included in City Sights Tour?

   A. Changi Airport

   B. Singapore Flyer

   C. Marina Bay Sands

   D. Gardens by the Bay

121

4. Which route is the woman recommended to choose?

   A. Heritage Tour

   B. City Sights Tour

   C. Both

   D. Neither

5. Which of the following is similar in meaning with the word "withstand"?

   A. To stand up

   B. To be different

   C. To make a contrast

   D. To go through

II. Listen to the following dialogue again and try to tell whether the following statements are true or not.

1. The woman plans to visit friends in Singapore. **(F)**

2. The city hall is newly built in the colonial district. **(F)**

3. The Merlion is a national symbol of Singapore. **(T)**

4. Two Tour routes take 2.5 hours long in all. **(F)**

5. City Sights Tour offers the night view of Singapore's famous icons along the Marina Bay. **(T)**

Part III Listening and Understanding

Dialogue: Unaccompanied Minor Lounges For Connection

Listen to the following dialogue and choose the proper answer to each question.

Tape scripts

Staff: Travel Centre. This is Steve Brent's speaking.

Passenger: Good morning, Mr. Brent. I've got a couple of questions to enquire about your unaccompanied minor service because my 12-year-old daughter is going to see her grandparents alone with Emirates Airlines.

Staff: What do you want to know about?

Passenger: What documents do I need to prepare?

Staff: At check-in, parents or guardians need to provide your daughter's birth certificate or passport as well as contact information of parents and the adult meeting your daughter at her destination. And you'll need to fill out an unaccompanied minor form and any necessary Customs and Immigration documents for the day of departure.

Passenger: All right, I've got it. And is there anyone taking care of my child during the connection?

Staff: We have lounges for unaccompanied minors supervised by a specialist member. Your daughter can play games or read with drinks and snacks while waiting.

Passenger: That'll be great! I'll set my mind to rest.

Staff: Is there anything else I can do?

Passenger: Not for now. Thank you very much and I really appreciate your time.

Staff: It's my pleasure. Don't hesitate to call us if you have any questions.

1. What kind of passengers does unaccompanied minor service apply to?

    A. National minorities

    B. People working for companies

    C. Children without their parents

    D. Children who travel alone

2. What documents do parents or guardians need to provide when checking-in?

    A. Child's birth certificate

    B. Parents' contact information

    C. Information of the adult meeting at destination

    D. All of the above.

3. Which of the following statements is not mentioned?

    A. Parents or guardians need to go through customs with their child.

    B. Parents or guardians need to provide their contact information.

    C. Her daughter is going to transfer at Dubai Airport.

    D. There are lounges for her daughter to rest during the connection.

4. What service is not included at the lounges for connection?

    A. A supervisor

    B. An airport tour

    C. Video games

    D. Drinks and snacks

5. What does the word "supervise" mean?

    A. To travel

    B. To provide

    C. To be responsible for

    D. To appreciate

Passage: A Transit Visa

I. Listen to the following passage and then choose the proper answer to each question.

Tape scripts

A transit visa is an entry permit for short stay which allows you to make a connection on your way to another country. Usually there are two types of transit visas: airport transit visa and visitor transit visa. An airport transit visa is generally valid for 48 hours and designated for holders to wait in the international transit area inside the airport. The latter one is granted to travelers who need to go out of the airport.

The restrictions or eligibility criteria are subject to change to certain conditions. And they are different depending on your nationality and destination country. For example, when traveling through a Schengen country, you don't need to apply for a transit Schengen visa if you are a family member of a citizen of the European Union, European Economic Area or Switzerland. Transit visa holders are permitted to stay in Australia for no longer than 72 hours, for less than 48 hours in Canada, no more than 5 days in Malaysia for Chinese holders. When applying for a transit visa in Thailand, Chinese people need to submit 2 application forms and 2 photographs but 4 application forms and 4 photographs for Iranian people.

1. When is a transit visa used for?

   A. To enter another country

   B. To leave another country

   C. To transfer through a country

   D. To go through an airport

2. Which of the following statements is not true?

   A. An airport transit visa holder can stay in the country for no more than 48 hours.

   B. A visitor transit visa holder can stay in the country as long as they can.

   C. An airport transit visa holder can stay within the airport.

   D. A visitor transit visa permits holders to go outside of the airport.

3. Which of the following statements is not mentioned here?

   A. A transit visa is free of charge.

   B. The restrictions are different.

   C. Each country has its own criteria on a transit visa.

   D. A transit visa application needs photographs in Thailand.

4. What does the word "eligibility" mean here?

   A. Transit

   B. Qualification

   C. Mobility

   D. Flexibility

5. Which of the following statements is true?

   A. A Schengen transit visa is needed for a citizen of EEA.

   B. Australian government permits transit visa holders to stay longer than 72 hours.

   C. Chinese people need to apply for a transit visa with 2 application forms and 4 photographs.

   D. The regulations and standards are different from country to country.

II. Listen again and make a correct order of the following sentences.

1. When traveling through a Schengen country, you don't need to apply for a transit Schengen visa if you are a family member of a citizen of the European Union.

2. Usually there are two types of transit visas: airport transit visa and visitor transit visa.

3. When applying for a transit visa in Thailand, Chinese people need to submit 2 application forms and 2 photographs.

4. The restrictions or eligibility criteria are subject to change to certain conditions.

5. The latter one is granted to travelers who need to go out of the airport.

Key: 2--5--4--1--3

Part IV   Listening and Enjoying

Recruitment

Listen to the following advertisement and then choose the proper answer to the questions.

Tape scripts

Air France is looking for a dynamic team player as In-flight commercial interpreter based in Guangzhou. You are responsible to act as a liaison officer and assist our Chinese customers on board.

Your Duties are:

➢ To promote Air France products and services through effective communication

➢ To assist the cabin crew and customers during the meal service and duty free sales on board.

➢ To provide regular customer feedback to the Chief Purser and your Line Manager.

➢ To perform all Chinese inflight announcements.

The job requires:

✧ Female, below 30 years old

✧ College degree or above

✧ Fluent in French and Mandarin, good command of English, Cantonese is a plus

✧ Excellent communication skills and team work

✧ Extensive knowledge in both Chinese and French culture is highly desirable

If you are interested in this position, please send your application via the website below before 17 June 2020.

1. What position is wanted?

   A. Tennis player

   B. Chinese attendant

   C. Inflight interpreter

   D. Chief purser

2. What duty is not mentioned?

A. To help crew with products and service

B. To promote the communication between customers and cabin crew

C. To provide customers' feedback to the chief purser

D. To work independently

3. What qualifications are required for the position?

A. Communication skills

B. Good command of French and Mandarin

C. University graduate

D. All of the above

4. Which of the following statements is not true?

A. The position is based in Guangzhou.

B. The applicant needs to be a female at thirties.

C. The applicant needs to know French culture.

D. The candidate had better send the application before the mid-June.

5. What does the word "plus" mean here?

A. Advantage

B. Application

C. Requirement

D. communication

Cultural Perspective: Iceland

Listen to the introduction to Iceland and fill in the missing words.

The Republic of Iceland is an island country in North Europe, and the Europe's second-largest island after Great Britain. One **1. eighth** of the country is covered with glaciers. The land is a bowl-like plateau surrounded with **2. mountains** and lava fields.

There are more than 100 **3. volcanoes** in Iceland, 40 to 50 of which are active ones. That is why Iceland is full of hot **4. springs**, beautiful colored rocks and other natural wonders. It's also known as A Country of Ice and Fire.

The **5. capital** is Reykjavik, a port city and also the largest city. Iceland has the smallest population in Europe. Historically, its economy depends heavily on fishing and **6. energy** supply. Legally, there is no standing army with a lightly armed Coast Guard. People here travel by road since there is no **7. passenger** railway, but a great number of roads are unpaved. Icelanders are among the world's healthiest people. The average life **8. expectancy** is 81.8, the 4th highest in the world.

Despite a high **9. latitude** just outside the Arctic Circle, Iceland has a temperate climate in winter because of the Gulf Stream, about -2°C in average. Visitors can experience **10. polar** days in summer or play snow locomotive or cross-country hunting in winter.

Unit 14   Customs and Quarantines

Part I   Pre-listening

Puzzles

Complete the following word puzzles according to the clues given below.

J	A	Z	Z
A			E
D			R
E	C	H	O

Up: a kind of popular music

Down: sound sent back

Left: hard green stone

Right: nought

Pronunciation

Listen and choose the right explanation of the sentences you hear.

1. Smith wants his sister to send a message to him.

    A. He wants to send a message.

    B. She wants to send a message.

    C. He wants a message from her.

2. The red necklace is less expensive than the blue one.

    A. The red one is cheaper.

    B. The red one is more expensive.

    C. They both cost the same.

3. Bill is watching TV while Susan is doing her homework.

    A. They are watching TV together.

    B. They are doing different things at the same time.

    C. Both of them are doing their homework.

4. Henry has been calling since 10 o'clock.

    A. He is calling at 10 o'clock.

    B. He is still calling now.

    C. He is not calling now.

5. Mike sings as well as Ellen.

    A. Ellen sings better.

    B. Mike sings better than Ellen.

    C. Both of them sing well.

6. Frank likes to go fishing but Emma prefers to go hiking.

   A. Frank likes fishing more than hiking.

   B. Emma likes fishing better.

   C. Emma likes both fishing and hiking.

7. The woman who came out of the office was a travel agent.

   A. A sales agent came out of the office.

   B. The woman was a travel agent.

   C. The woman came out of the agent's office.

8. I don't know the actor they are talking about.

   A. They're talking about an actor.

   B. They are talking about me.

   C. I really know what they are talking about.

Part II   Listening In

Responses

You will hear five sentences. Listen carefully and select the best response to the question or statement.

1. Do you have anything to declare, Sir?

   A. No, you don't have to.

   B. Yes, I'm Mr. Claire.

   C. I don't think so.

2. Please fill out the form on your left.

   A. Sure, I'll do it now.

   B. I got out of the farm.

   C. I left the case at home.

3. What time are we supposed to meet Mr. Black?

   A. At the back of the building.

   B. Around ten o'clock, I think.

   C. I think he is in the meeting now.

4. Are we going to have a seminar this afternoon?

   A. I'll see you this afternoon.

   B. It's been rescheduled for tomorrow.

   C. No, it's out of service.

5. Do you want me to drive you to the airport?

   A. I have turned in my report.

   B. I'll travel first class.

   C. If you don't mind.

Questions: General Information about CIQ

You will hear some sentences. Listen carefully and select the best response to the question.

Tape scripts

1. All arriving and departing international passengers are required to complete a customs declaration form, an immigration declaration card and a travelers quarantine system(C.I.Q).

How many channels are there at an airport?

A. customs

B. immigration

C. quarantine

D. above all

2. Immigration controls and checks people entering and leaving the country in order to keep the public order in that country. Customs control the outflow and inflow of the currency and products. Quarantine is the system which is set up to check people, plants and animals, aircraft and cargo for infectious disease.

What is the function of Customs?

A. To control the outflow and inflow of the currency and products.

B. To control and check people entering and leaving the country.

C. To check people, plants and animals, aircraft and cargo for infectious disease.

D. Above all

3. At most airports all over the world, there are normally the Red Channel and Green Channel to exit through customs. The former refers to "Goods to Declare" channel; the latter refers to "Nothing to Declare".

How many exits are there to go through customs?

A. 1

B. 2

C. 3

D. 4

4. Quarantine can be divided into: human quarantine, plant quarantine and animal quarantine.

How many categories can quarantine be divided into?

A. 1

B. 2

C. 3

D. 4

5. Flight crew will present their passports to the immigration officer and have him put check marks to the left of their names on the General Declaration and Crew Manifest (G/D for short).

Where will the immigration officer mark his check on flight crew's passport?

A. On the right of their names

B. On the left of their names

C. On the upside of their names

D. On the downside of their names

Dialogue: My Customs Declaration

Listen to the following dialogue and choose the proper answer to the question.

Tape scripts

Customs Agent: May I see your luggage?

PAX: Yes, certainly.

CA: Will you please open that large suitcase?

PAX: Sure.

CA: Do you have anything other than personal effects in here?

PAX: Well, I do have a few gifts.

CA: What kind of gifts?

PAX: Well, I have one watch, two cartons of cigarettes, a box of cigars, and some silk cloth.

CA: I'm afraid you'll have to pay duty on the watch, and on either one carton of cigarettes or a box of cigars.

PAX: I thought I could take in two cartons of cigarettes and a box of cigars duty free.

CA: No, you're limited to 200 cigarettes and 25 cigars. Anything above that is subjected to duty.

PAX: How much will the duty be on the watch and the cigars?

CA: Let me see. Altogether it will be 25 dollars. I'll make out a statement and take it over to the cashier. After you get your things together, you can pay over there.

PAX: Thank you.

1. Which item did he not buy?

    A. cigar

    B. perfume

    C. cognac

    D. cloth

2. What's the limitation of the cigarettes and cigars?

    A. 25 cigarettes and 200 cigars

    B. 200 cigarettes and 25 cigars

    C. 1 box of cigars and 2 cartons of cigarettes

    D. 2 boxes of cigars and 1 carton of cigarettes.

3. Which items did he choose to pay at last?

Keys and Audio scripts

A. watch and cloth

B. 1 carton of cigarettes and a box of cigars

C. watch and cigars

D. cigars and cloth

4. Which of the following statements is true?

A. He had nothing to declare.

B. He bought some wine as gifts.

C. He paid the duty to the customs agent.

D. He carried a few gifts as well as his personal belongings.

Dialogue: China Immigration Clearance

Listen to the dialogue and complete the information in the card.

Immigration Officer: Excuse me, sir? where are you from?

PAX: My father is a Chinese, but mother is an Austrian. My nationality is **Austria.**

IO: Please give me the arrival card to enter China.

PAX: All right. Here it is. My name is **Tom Li**.

IO: Please give me your Passport as well….

PAX: Sure. Here you are, the place of visa issuance is **Sydney.**

IO: Hmm, passport number…**L8846370**, OK, what's your flight number and the purpose of your visit?

PAX: My flight number is **CA 2323**. I'm coming to **visit my friends**. Today is 9th Oct. 2019. It's my 26th **birthday today.** I've booked a party room at **Hilton Hotel**.

IO: Happy birthday, you may leave.

ARRIVAL CARD 外国人入境卡

Family name 姓	Li	Given names 名: Tom
Nationality 国籍	Austria	Passport No. 护照号码: L8846370
Intended Address in China 在华住址	Hilton Hotel	Male ☑ Female ☐
Date of birth 出生日期	Year 1993 Month 10 Day 9	Purpose of visit (one only) 入境事由
Visa No. 签证号码		Conference/Business ☐ Visit ☐ Sightseeing/in leisure ☐
Place of Visa Issuance 签证签发地	Sydney	Visiting friends or relatives ☑ Employment ☐ Study ☐
Flight No./Ship's name/Train No. 航班号/船名/车次	CA 2323	Return home ☐ Settle down ☐ Others ☐

以上申明真实准确。
I hereby declare that the statement given above is true and accurate.

Signature 签名 _____

Part III Listening and Understanding

Passage: Peoples Republic of China Duty Free Allowances Summary

Listen to the following passage and choose the proper answer to the question.

China (PRC) Duty Free For travel to mainland China when your stay is less than 6 months your duty free allowance is:

• 400 cigarettes

• Two bottles (up to 75cl each) of alcohol.

• A reasonable amount of perfume for personal use.

• 50g of gold or silver.

• Personal effects for your own use are duty free.

• Gifts and presents must be declared.

For stays in excess of 6 months these allowances rise to: 600 Cigarettes and four 75cl bottles of spirits.

Please also make sure you complete a passenger luggage declaration form on arrival. Ensure that you list all valuables e.g. jewellery, cameras, watches and anything else of value as this must be presented and checked on departure.

Keep ALL receipts for valuable items and effects you buy while in China so you can obtain your export certificate from the authorities when you leave.

1. Which city do these rules apply to?

   A. Hangzhou

   B. Taiwan

   C. Hong Kong

   D. Macau

2. How many cigarettes differences you can take when your stay is less than 6 months and excess of 6 months?

   A. 400

   B. 600

   C. 1200

   D. 200

3. You need to pay for the duty if you're taking _____ out of China.

   A. A 50cl bottle of spirits for stays within 6 months

   B. 5kg of silver for stays within 6 months

   C. 400 cigarettes for stays more than 6 months

   D. 2x75cl bottles of alcoholic for stays more than 6 months

4. Which of the following statements is correct?

   A. Things for personal use are duty free.

B. Gifts must not be declared.

C. Valuable items must be checked if you don't complete the luggage declaration form.

D. Keep all receipts for valuable effects when entering China.

5. Which of the following statements is not correct?

A. Make sure you complete a passenger luggage declaration form on arrival.

B. Keep ALL receipts for valuable items and effects you buy while in China.

C. For stays in excess of 6 months, you can bring two bottles of alcoholic.

D. You can bring a reasonable amount of perfume for personal use no matter how many months you stay.

Passage: Macau Duty Free Allowances Summary

Listen to the following passage and fill the form about the allowances of each item.

Tape scripts

While both Macau and Hong Kong are Special Administrative Regions of the Peoples Republic of China, they both have their own Customs policies, regulations and allowances. Travelling between them is deemed as international travel and so is subject to immigration procedures and customs checks.

Macau Duty Free Visitors to Macau may bring in duty and tax free items to the value of 10,000 MOP (Macau Pataca) – as a guide this is the equivalent to $1240 (USD) or €900 (Euros) or £780 (GBP Sterling). Personal duty free allowances on the following are: 19 cigarettes or 1 cigar or 25 grams of other manufactured tobacco,1 litre of spirits (exceeding 30% abv), 1 litre of wine (not exceeding 30% abv), clothes, jewelry, sports equipment and 1 personal computer for private use. Other items are not restricted nor subject to import duties, providing they are in reasonable quantities and for personal use only.

Macau has no export duties and so any gifts or presents purchased will not be subject to tax.

Items	Allowance
Alcoholic liquor/spirit with an alcoholic strength above 30% (liter)	**1 litre**
Cigarettes	**19 cigarettes**
Manufactured Tobacco (grams)	**25g**
Jewelry	**Reasonable quantities for personal use**
computer	**1 for personal use**
Cigar	**1**

Listen to the passage again and answer the following questions.

1. Why is traveling from China mainland to Macau subject to customs check?

Because travelling between China mainland and Macau is deemed as international travel.

2. Write down all the duty free items which are mentioned in this passage.

Cigarettes, cigar, tobacco, spirit, wine, clothes, jewelry ,sports equipment, personal computer

3. On what condition are other items not restricted to import?

Provided that these items are in reasonable quantities and for personal use.

4. How much tax free of the items you may bring in Macau?(MOP)

10,000MOP

5. Why all the gifts and presents purchased will not be subject to tax?

Macau has no export duties.

Part IV Listening and Enjoying

Passage: European airlines

Listen to the following passage and choose the proper answer to the question.

Tape scripts

Each European airline maintains its own individual style and cultural identity. At the same time each airline shares a common dedication to the highest standards of safety and customer service.

Safety is always a top priority for all airlines. It's the fundamental guarantee to all service, otherwise everything is empty.

It is reported that flights from European airlines are in a high punctual rate. "Punctuality" is most frequently mentioned from interview to board training.

Details determine one's fate. Detail is the right fit to cabin service. For instance, logos on the cups are put in the same direction.

Flight attendants in European airlines are famous to be professional, dynamic and pleasant in manner, making passengers quite comfortable. Airlines value on attendants' abilities in problem-solving, acting with a positive attitude, and cooperating with colleagues. On the other hand, European airlines like attendants to show their individuality based on general standards.

1. Which of the following statements is correct?

    A. Each European airline has the same service standard.

    B. Every flight from European airlines is punctual.

    C. Passengers feel comfortable with European attendants' service.

    D. European airlines don't like their attendants to show any individuality.

2. What service standards in European airlines are similar?

    A. Punctuality

    B. Safety

    C. Eyes on details

    D. All of the above.

3. What does "priority" mean in the second paragraph?

A. importance

   B. attempt

   C. possibility

   D. direction

4. What does the fact show that logos on the cups are put in the same direction?

   A. European airlines are strict to their attendants.

   B. European airlines pay much attention to the detail in their service.

   C. European people like drinking tea.

   D. European attendants show their individuality in this way.

5. European airlines value their attendants on the following abilities except_____.

   A. Positive attitude

   B. Cooperation

   C. Team work

   D. Individuality above general standards

Culture Perspective: Hulun Buir Grassland

Listen to the following passage and fill in the missing words.

Tape scripts

Hulun Buir Grassland situates in the west of Greater Xing'an Mountains, **covering** an area of about 100,000 square kilometers. Natural grassland accounts for 80% of this area. It has been called "**the cradle** of Chinese northern nomadic people".

Hulun Buir Grassland is famous for its beautiful scenery and rich **natural** resources. There are more beautiful things than the eye can **take in**: twisting river, Mongolian yurts, shrubs, blue sky, herds of cattle and sheep on the **endless** grassland. It feels like a **relaxing** and refreshing picture. Winters here are quite long and bitterly cold with heavy ice and snow, while summers are temperate and comfortably cool. It's **worthy** of the title of summer resort.

Visitors can watch **performances** with local features, like wrestling, dancing or Barhu wedding(a traditional Mongolian wedding ceremony). You can also try the daily activities such as milking cows, shearing sheep or **boiling** milk tea, etc.

It is also a place where visitors can experience the **unique** customs and cultures of ethnic groups like Ewenk, Orogen, Daur and Russian minorities.

Bibliography

[1] Harry Collis, Joe Kohl. 美国谜语 101 则[M]. 北京：外语教学与研究出版社，2004.

[2] Simon Greenall, 文秋芳. 新标准大学英语文化阅读教程[M]. 北京：外语教学与研究出版社，2012.

[3] 李燕，徐静. 旅游英语[M]. 北京：清华大学出版社，2009.

[4] 黄振泽. 幽默英语名言[M]. 北京：科学出版社，2011.

[5] 金利. 旅游英语拿起就会——TOP200 旅游情景会话一本搞定[M]. 上海：华东理工大学出版社，2015.

[6] 李然. 零基础新手马上开口说出国旅游英语[M]. 北京：中国宇航出版社，2014.

[7] 李勇. 新编民航乘务员实用英语[M]. 北京：中国民航出版社，2009.

[8] 尹静. 民航地勤英语[M]. 北京：北京大学出版社，2008.

[9] 蔡文宜. 带着英语就出发，我的海外旅行[M]. 北京：化学工业出版社，2015.

[10] 董何. 一幽一默人生无难事[M]. 北京：中国纺织出版社，2010.

[11] 郝向利，滕京. 实用文化英语[M]. 武汉：武汉大学出版社，2012.

[12] 潘水明. 航空商务英语[M]. 北京：国防工业出版社，2007.

[13] 盛湘君. 英语实训教程——视听说（进阶篇）[M]. 杭州：浙江大学出版社，2009.

Appendix

国际主要航空公司名称及代码

航空公司名称	两字码/三字码	标　　识
奥凯航空公司 OK AIRLINES	BK/OKA	
澳门航空公司 AIR MACAU	NX/AMU	
港龙航空公司 DRAGON AIR	KA/HDA	
长龙航空公司 LOONG AIR	GJ/CDC	
春秋航空公司 SPRING AIRLINES	9C/CQH	
大连航空公司 DALIAN AIRLINES	CA/CCD	
吉祥航空 JUNEYAO AIRLINES	HO/DKH	
九元航空公司 9AIR CO., LTD.	AQ/JYH	
昆明航空公司 KUNMING AIRLINES	KY/KNA	
山东航空公司（中国） SHANDONG AIRLINES	SC/CDG	
上海航空公司 SHANGHAI AIRLINES	FM/CSH	
深圳航空公司 SHENZHEN AIRLINES	ZH/CSZ	
首都航空公司 CAPITAL AIRLINES CO., LTD.	JD/CBJ	
四川航空公司 SICHUAN AIRLINES	3U/CSC	
天津航空公司 TIANJIN AIRLINES	GS/GCR	

续表

航空公司名称	两字码/三字码	标　　识
武汉航空公司 CHINA WUHAN AIRLINES	WU/CWU	
西藏航空公司 TIBET AIRLINES CO., LTD.	TV/TBA	
厦门航空有限公司 XIAMEN AIRLINES	MF/CXA	
祥鹏航空 LUCKY AIR	8L/LKE	
新疆航空公司 XINJIANG AIRLINES	XO/CXJ	
幸福航空 JOY AIR	JR/JOY	
中国北方航空公司 CHINA NORTHERN AIRLINES	CJ/CBJ	
中国东方航空公司 CHINA EASTERN AIRLINES	MU/CES	
中国国际航空公司 AIR CHINA	CA/CCA	
海南航空公司 HAINAN AIRLINES	HU/CHH	
中国长安航空公司 CHANG'AN AIRLINES	2Z/CGN	
中国长城航空公司 AIR GREAT WALL	G8/GWL	
中国联合航空公司 CHINA UNITED AIRLINES	KN/CUA	
中国南方航空公司 CHINA SOUTHERN AIRLINES	CZ/CSN	

续表

航空公司名称	两字码/三字码	标　　识
中国西南航空公司 CHINA SOUTHWEST AIRLINES	SZ/CXN	
中国邮政航空公司 CHINA POSTAL AIRLINES	CF/CYZ	
阿尔及利亚航空公司 AIR ALGERIE	AH/DAH	
阿根廷航空公司 AEROLINES ARGENTINAS	AR/ARG	
阿联酋航空 EMIRATES AIRLINE	EK/UAE	
阿拉伯利比亚航空公司 LYBIAN ARAB AIRLINES	LN/LAA	
阿提哈德航空公司 ETIHAD AIRWAYS	EY/ETD	
埃及航空公司 EGYPT AIR	MS/MSR	
埃塞俄比亚航空公司 ETHIOPIAN AIRLINES CORPORATION	ET/ETH	
安哥拉航空公司 ANGOLA AIRLINES	DT/DTA	
奥地利航空公司 AUSTRIAN AIRLINES	OS/AUA	
奥林匹克航空公司（希腊） OLYMPIC AIRWAYS S.A.	OA/OAL	
巴哈马航空公司（巴哈马） BAHAMASAIR HOLDINGS LTD.	UP/BHS	
巴基斯坦国际航空公司 PAKISTAN INTERNATIONAL AIRLINES (PIA)	PK/PIA	

Appendix

续表

航空公司名称	两字码/三字码	标　　识
巴拉圭航空公司 LINEAS AEREAS PARAGUAYAS	PZ/LAP	
巴拿马国际航空公司 PANAMA AIR INTERNATIONAL	CM/CMP	
柏林航空公司（德国） AIR BERLIN,INC.	AB/BER	
北欧航空公司（瑞典） SCANDINAVIAN AIRLINES SYSTEM	SK/SAS	
波兰航空公司 POLISH AIRLINES	LO/LOT	
大韩航空公司（韩国） KOREAN AIR	KE/KAL	
俄罗斯国际航空公司 RUSSIAN AIRLINES	SU/ALF	
法国航空公司 AIR FRANCE	AF/AFR	
菲律宾航空公司 PHILIPPINE AIRLINES	PR/PAL	
芬兰航空公司 FINNAIR	AY/FIN	
哈萨克斯坦航空公司 AIR KAZAKHSTAN	K4/KZR	
汉莎航空公司（德国） DEUTSCHE LUFTHANSA	LH/DLH	
韩亚航空 ASIANA AIRLINES	OZ/AAR	
荷兰皇家航空公司 K.L.M.ROYAL DUTCH AIRLINES	KL/KLM	

续表

航空公司名称	两字码/三字码	标　　识
加拿大航空公司 AIR CANADA	AC/ACA	
捷克航空公司 CZECH AIRLINES J.S.C.	OK/CSA	
卡塔尔航空公司 QATAR AIRWAYS	QR/QTR	
科威特航空公司 KUWAIT AIRWAYS CORPORATION	KU/KAC	
肯尼亚航空公司 KENYA AIRWAYS, LTD.	KQ/KQA	
斯里兰卡航空公司 SRILANKA AIRLINES	UL/ALK	
卢旺达航空公司 RWANDA AIR	WB/RWD	
马耳他航空有限公司 AIR MALTA CO., LTD.	KM/AMC	
新加坡酷航空公司 SCOOT AIRLINES	TZ/SCO	
马来西亚航空公司 MALAYSIAN AIRLINES SYSTEM	MH/MAS	
美国航空公司 AMERICAN AIRLINES INC.	AA/AAL	American Airlines
毛里求斯航空公司 AIR MAURITIUS	MK/MAU	AIR MAURITIUS
缅甸航空公司 MYANMA AIRWAYS	UB/UBA	

续表

航空公司名称	两字码/三字码	标　　识
南非航空公司 SOUTH AFRICAN AIRWAYS	SA/SAA	
尼泊尔皇家航空公司 ROYAL NEPAL AIRLINES	RA/RNA	
意大利航空公司 ALITALIA	AZ/AZA	
全日空航空有限公司（日本） ALL NIPPON AIRWAYS	NH/ANA	
日本航空公司 JAPAN AIRLINES Corp.	JL/JAL	
瑞士航空公司 SWISSAIR	SR/SWR	
塞浦路斯航空有限公司 CYPRUS AIRWAYS LTD.	CY/CYP	
世界航空公司（美国） WORLD AIRWAYS INC.	WO/WOA	
坦桑尼亚航空公司 AIR TANZANIA	TC/ATC	
突尼斯航空公司 TUNIS AIR	TU/TAR	TUNISAIR
土耳其航空公司 TURKISH AIRLINES CO.	TK/THY	TURKISH AIRLINES TÜRK HAVA YOLLARI
文莱皇家航空公司 BRUNEI AIRLINES	BI/RBA	ROYAL BRUNEI
乌克兰国际航空公司 UKRAINE INTERNATIONAL AIRLINES	PS/UIA	
新加坡航空公司 SINGAPORE AIRLINES	SQ/SIA	SINGAPORE AIRLINES
新西兰航空有限公司 AIR NEW ZEALAND	NZ/ANZ	

续表

航空公司名称	两字码/三字码	标　识
匈牙利航空公司 MALEV-HUNGARIAN AIRLINES	MA/MAH	
牙买加航空公司 AIR JAMAICA	JM/AJM	airJamaica
伊拉克航空公司 IRAQI AIRWAYS	IA/IAW	
伊朗航空公司 IRAN AIR	IR/IRA	
以色列航空有限公司 EL AL-ISRAEL AIRLINES	LY/ELY	
印度航空公司 AIR INDIAN	AI/AIC	AIR INDIA
印度尼西亚鹰航 GARUDA INDONESIA AIRLINE	GA/GIA	
英国航空公司 BRITISH AIRWAYS	BA/BAW	BRITISH AIRWAYS